The German Länder

Werner Reutter

The German Länder

An Introduction

Werner Reutter
Institut für Sozialwissenschaften
Humboldt-Universität zu Berlin
Berlin, Germany

ISBN 978-3-658-33680-6   ISBN 978-3-658-33681-3   (eBook)
https://doi.org/10.1007/978-3-658-33681-3

This book is a translation of the original German edition „Die deutschen Länder" by Reutter, Werner, published by Springer Fachmedien Wiesbaden GmbH in 2020. The translation was done with the help of artificial intelligence (machine translation by the service DeepL.com). A subsequent human revision was done primarily in terms of content, so that the book will read stylistically differently from a conventional translation. Springer Nature works continuously to further the development of tools for the production of books and on the related technologies to support the authors.

Responsible Editor: Jan Treibel
This Springer imprint is published by the registered company Springer Fachmedien Wiesbaden GmbH part of Springer Nature.
The registered company address is: Abraham-Lincoln-Str. 46, 65189 Wiesbaden, Germany

Preface to the English Edition

This is the English version of a textbook about the German *Länder*. It is an offspring of my research interest on German federalism and its constituent units, the Länder. In fact, I studied the Länder, some of their policies, their institutions and how they fit into the overall political system of Germany for some time and found that they deserve an introduction that can be used by students and all those interested in this subject in Germany.

Even though there are a number of books on German federalism also in English there is no up-to-date overview on the German Länder. With this book I try to provide such an overview and introduce a topic which I find deserves greater interest also abroad. In order to disseminate my findings also to a wider audience in other countries, my publisher, Springer VS, offered me the chance to participate in a larger project in which artificial intelligence comes into play. Springer VS cooperated with DeepL an online tool for translations. Deepl made a first translation of the original text.

However, I took some liberties in correcting and adjusting the translated version provided by DeepL.com to make the book more accessible to readers not familiar with the details and intricacies of German federalism and German Länder. This included also some decisions on terms. In many cases, I retained the German term instead of replacing it with its English twin. E.g. throughout the book I talk about the *Länder* even though subnational units very often are called "states" like in the USA. However, this would have been rather confusing as we use the term "state" in Germany to refer to what Americans or English people would call government. With regard to German quotes, I mostly translated them into English. However, if it seemed more sensible I left out the quotation marks but kept, of course, the reference.

Contents

1 Introduction: The German *Länder* Between Diversity and Unity 1
  1.1 Introduction, or What this Book is About 1
  1.2 Outline and Objectives of the Book........................ 3

2 The *Länder*: How they Became what they are 7
  2.1 Prehistory: The *Länder* Between the End and Beginning 7
  2.2 *Land* Borders: Reorganization, Mergers,
       Accessions and German Unification 17
  2.3 Equivalent Living Conditions, Unitarism and Differences:
       Society, Economy and Culture in the *Länder* 20

3 Federalism and *Länder*: Basic Constitutional Principles and Theories 25
  3.1 Basic Law, the *Länder,* and German Federalism 25
  3.2 *Land* Constitutions: The Political Orders in the *Länder* 29
  3.3 *Länder* and Federalism: Theoretical Approaches 34

4 Representative and Direct Democracy in the *Länder*: Complement or Contradiction?................................. 37
  4.1 Elections and Democracy in the *Länder* 37
  4.2 Direct Democracy in the *Länder* 44

5 Parties and Party Systems in the *Länder* 49
  5.1 The Status of Parties in the *Länder* 49
  5.2 Tasks of Parties in the *Länder* 51
  5.3 Party Systems in the *Länder:* Structures and Development. 52

6 Parliaments, Governments and Constitutional Courts: Division of Powers in the *Länder*............................. 59
  6.1 Division of Powers in the *Länder* 59
  6.2 *Land* Parliaments: The Legislative Power 60
      6.2.1 Structure and Mode of Operation...................... 61
      6.2.2 Tasks: "Talking and Acting" 63

6.3   *Land* Governments and *Land* Administrations:
       The Executive Power   69
       6.3.1   Structure and Mode of Operation.   69
       6.3.2   Tasks: Steering and Directing   72
6.4   *Land* Constitutional Courts: The Judicial Power   75
       6.4.1   Structure and Mode of Operation.   77
       6.4.2   Tasks: Constitution and Politics.   79

7   **The *Länder*, the Federation, and Europe**   81
     7.1   The *Bundesrat:* The Chamber of the *Länder*
            within the Federation   81
     7.2   Horizontal and Vertical Coordination:
            The *Länder* in the Federation and in Europe   86

8   **The *Länder*, Democracy, and Federalism in Germany**   91

Annotated Literature   93

References   95

Abbreviations

AfD	Alternative for Germany (Alternative für Deutschland)
AL	Alternative List for Democracy and Environmental Protection (Alternative Liste für Demokratie und Umweltschutz)
Art.	Article
BAV	Bavaria (Bayern)
BB	Brandenburg
BER	Berlin
BL	Basic Law (Grundgesetz)
BRE	Bremen
BVB/Freie Wähler	Brandenburg United Civic Movements/Free Voters (Brandenburger Vereinigte Bürgerbewegungen/Freie Wähler)
BW	Baden-Württemberg
CDU	Christian Democratic Union of Germany (Christlich Demokratische Union Deutschlands)
CSU	Christian Social Union in Bavaria (Christlich-Soziale Union in Bayern)
DVP	Democratic People's Party (Demokratische Volkspartei)
DVU	German People's Union (Deutsche Volksunion)
EU	European Union (Europäische Union)
FDP	Free Democratic Party (Freie Demokratische Partei)
FRG	Federal Republic of Germany (Bundesrepublik Deutschland)
FW	Party of Free Voters (Freie Wähler)
GAL	Green-Alternative List (Grün-Alternative Liste)
GDP	Gross Domestic Product
GDR	German Democratic Republic (Deutsche Demokratische Republik)
HAM	Hamburg
HES	Hesse (Hessen)
KPD	Communist Party of Germany (Kommunistische Partei Deutschlands)

LDP	Liberal Democratic Party of Hesse (Liberal-Demokratische Partei Hessen)
LS	Lower Saxony (Niedersachsen)
MPC	Minister Presidents' Conference (Ministerpräsidentenkonferenz)
MP	Member of Parliament
MW	Mecklenburg-Western Pomerania (Mecklenburg-Vorpommern)
NGOs	Non-governmental organizations
NPD	National Democratic Party of Germany (Nationaldemokratische Partei Deutschlands)
NRW	North Rhine-Westphalia (Nordrhein-Westfalen)
PDS	Party of Democratic Socialism (Partei des Demokratischen Sozialismus)
RP	Rhineland-Palatinate (Rheinland-Pfalz)
SAT	Saxony-Anhalt (Sachsen-Anhalt)
SAY	Saxony (Sachsen)
SED	Socialist Unity Party of Germany (Sozialistische Einheitspartei Deutschlands)
SED-W	Socialist Unity Party of West-Berlin (Sozialistische Einheitspartei Westberlins)
SEW	Socialist Unity Party of West-Berlin (Sozialistische Einheitspartei Westberlins)
SH	Schleswig-Holstein (Schleswig-Holstein)
SLD	Saarland (Saarland)
SMAD	Soviet Military Administration (Sowjetische Militäradministration in Deutschland)
SPD	Social Democratic Party of Germany (Sozialdemokratische Partei Deutschlands)
SSW	South Schleswig Voters' Association (Südschleswigscher Wählerverband)
TH	Thuringia (Thüringen)
UK	United Kingdom (Vereinigtes Königreich)
Wrttbg.-Baden	Württemberg-Baden
Wrttbg.-Hohenzollern	Württemberg-Hohenzollern

Introduction: The German *Länder* Between Diversity and Unity

1

Abstract

The textbook looks at German federalism from the perspective of the Länder. The first Chapter introduces the topic and explains the concept of the federal state. In addition, the structure of the book is presented.

1.1   Introduction, or What this Book is About

If surveys are to be believed, *Länder* and federalism are not particularly popular in Germany. In 2007, the Bertelsmann Stiftung asked a total of 4,015 people whether they thought the *Länder* were dispensable "because the federal government and the European Union would deal with the really important issues". One in four respondents "tended to agree" with this statement and considered the *Länder* to be "superfluous" or "dispensable" (Bertelsmann Stiftung, 2008, p. 16). Moreover, just a minority of Germany's inhabitants can identify with a specific *Land*. Only around 11%—in other surveys, the figures were 12 and 13%, respectively—said they felt "primarily" affiliated with the *Land* in which the respondent resided at the time of the survey (Bertelsmann Stiftung, 2008, p. 13; Köcher, 2012, p. 761; Petersen, 2019, p. 124). Europe even seems closer to people than their own *Land*. For in both surveys, 14 and 17%, respectively, felt European. The federal state thus seems to have little "charisma" (Grube, 2009, p. 160; Petersen, 2019).

However, skepticism towards the *Länder* and federalism is not only part of public opinion. It is also widespread in political science. Fritz W. Scharpf, one of the most distinguished experts—and harshest critics—of German federalism, stated soberly in 2009 that there was federalism in the Federal Republic of Germany, but no federalists (Scharpf, 2009, p. 117). By this Scharpf meant that the *Länder* would hardly even make use of the few competencies that remained to them. Much rather than using competencies "autonomously", the *Länder* would seek uniform federal solutions by way of self-coordination (Scharpf, 2009, p. 117). Ten years later, the former Minister of Science, Economics and Transport of Schleswig–Holstein Dietrich Austermann was no less exasperated. He even proposed to "abolish the *Länder*" because this is not how federalism was meant to be! According to Austermann, the *Länder* had been virtually deprived of almost all legislative competencies. In addition, German federalism lacked a clear separation of financial and decision-making powers between the federal government and the *Länder*. Finally, *Land* parliaments need to have a greater say in policy-making (Austermann, 2019, p. 434). If the Basic Law did not prohibit it in the eternity clause, we should simply bid farewell to the *Länder* and thus to federalism (Austermann, 2019, p. 437).

So, political science and public opinion seem to agree: The *Länder* in the Federal Republic of Germany are meaningless because everything is (or should be) decided at the national level or by the EU. Moreover, German cooperative federalism is considered ineffective because decisions take too long and produce mostly second- or third-best common denominator solutions among the 16 *Länder* and the federal government. And citizens apparently do not seem to care anyway whether they live in a federal republic or in a unitary state.

But (and this is a big "but"): citizens are by no means only dissatisfied with their *Länder*. For example, in the survey by the Institute for Public Opinion Research (*Institut für Demoskopie*) quoted above, for example, 75% of respondents had been born in the *Land* in which they lived. And of the 25% who had moved to another *Land*, more than half had lived in their new home for 25 years or more (Köcher, 2012, p. 761). Regional ties and a sense of belonging may also be the reasons why there have been only a few attempts so far to at least partially heed Austermann's call and merge *Länder*. Since the Federal Republic of Germany came into existence, there have only been two such attempts. The first was successful in 1952 and led to the the the *Land* known as Baden-Württemberg that still exists today; the second failed because in 1996 the majority of Brandenburgers did not want to merge with the heavily indebted city-state of Berlin. It seems, then, that the *Länder* have an astonishing power to endure and to retain their inhabitants for a long time. Hans-Georg Wehling (2006, p. 7) also points out that politics in the *Länder* plays a "central role" in the "everyday lives of the people". The *Länder* are important because of their "substantive responsibilities" (ibid.). Finally, it should be mentioned that in an international comparison, the Federal Republic of Germany is classified as decidedly federal and decentralized (Lijphart, 1999, pp. 186–191; Krumm, 2015, p. 165).

One subject—two views. These are good prerequisites for taking a closer look at the German *Länder*, especially since citizens—as shown, for example, by the Bertelsmann survey (2008)—are only partially aware of the possibilities and limits of *Land* politics. The textbook wants to remedy this deficiency. It is intended to provide an insight into and information about the German *Länder*, their history, their constitutional foundations, their political systems, and how they are embedded into the overall political order of the Federal Republic of Germany. First, however, the structure of the textbook is to be explained.

1.2 Outline and Objectives of the Book

A federal state is "an amalgamation of several state organizations and legal systems, namely those of the constituent states [*Gliedstaaten*] endowed with their own powers and those of the state as a whole" (Vogel, 1995, p. 1043). According to this definition, the Federal Republic of Germany is a federal state, because it consists of a federation (the central state) and 16 member states (the German *Länder*). A federal state differs from a unitary state (such as France), because the latter only knows a "uniform state organization and single legal system", and from a confederation of states because this fails to form a unity (Vogel, 1995, p. 1043). In other words, distinct from a federal state, a unitary state lacks (legal) diversity, while a confederation lacks (legal) unity.

The presentation is oriented towards this pair of concepts: Diversity and unity. The two terms are used to describe federal states in general and German federalism in particular. In federal orders, the diversity of member states is to be preserved and, at the same time, the unity of the state as a whole is to be guaranteed. Even from this rather general description it becomes clear that a federal construction can (and should) lead to tensions. For such a construction gives rise to a whole series of necessities and constraints which make conflicts between member states and the central state almost inevitable. Typical questions in this context are: Which tasks has the central state to perform and which subnational units? What rights do the member states (in our case, the *Länder*) have? And what duties do they have, vis-à-vis the state as a whole? How are conflicts between the federal government and the states (*Länder*), but also between states, resolved? How do the constituent states participate in the decision-making process of the central state? In federal states such as the USA, Switzerland, Austria or the Federal Republic of Germany, all these questions find different answers (Krumm, 2015).

Research on federalism in Germany focuses primarily on the relationship between the federal government and the *Länder*. Studies grappling with this issue thus focus on one dimension of German federalism: the formation of unity. In this perspective, the *Länder* are understood as components in the structure of the polity. Their political, cultural, economic, or social diversity is often regarded as less important or even neglected. This is as evident in Austermann's polemic as it is in the concept of the "unitary federal state" (Hesse, 1962), or in the claim that we live in a "disguised unitary state" (Abromeit, 1992). And this dimension is also referred to again and again in the further presentation.

Anyone who has ever moved from Bavaria to Bremen, or from Bremen to Bavaria may wonder how this can be. After all, the school systems and the quality of the schools differ between the two *Länder* just as much as the administrations, the economic power or the religious commitment of the inhabitants. And legal scholars and lawyers who deal with administrative law, for example, complain about the variety of regulations and differences between the *Länder* (Winterhoff, 2012).

In the following, we also look at German federalism from the perspective of the *Länder*. This textbook is therefore not primarily concerned with federalism, to which the adjective "cooperative" is usually attached because the *Länder* and the federal government have to work together in various forms. Rather, the German *Länder* are the subject of the presentation. Their role in and significance for the democratic federal state are to be described and analysed. The diversity of the *Länder* is emphasized, and the differences as well as the commonalities between the *Länder* are elaborated. This includes social and economic dimensions (Chap. 2), as well as political and constitutional foundations (Chaps. 3–6).

First of all, a misunderstanding must be avoided. *Länder* are not to be equated with regions, as can be found in other member states in the European Union. The German *Länder* are unique in a European comparison. The EU does not recognize the *Länder*, and its treaties never mention *Länder* but only know regions. As is well known, only a minority of EU member states have a federal structure. According to our understanding of federalism, only Belgium, Austria and the Federal Republic of Germany qualify as federal states. Some also consider Spain to be an "inauthentic" federal state (Krumm, 2015). And some believe federalism is just a state organizational principle anyway, which merely gives special importance to decentralized units. In this perspective, federalism is hardly different from regionalism in the French unitary state, or devolution in the UK's asymmetric federal state. The rest of the account is based on a different understanding. In the foreground is the question of whether and to what extent German federalism provides the conditions for "political self-determination", i.e. for democracy, in the *Länder*. In other words, it is a question that addresses the democratic quality of German federalism, insofar as this quality manifests itself at the level of the *Länder*. *Länder* are regarded as elements of the democratic order of the Federal Republic of Germany.

The further presentation takes place in seven steps. The second chapter provides information on the 16 *Länder*. It gives an overview of the origins of the *Länder*, of their development and of central economic, social and cultural characteristics. The third chapter examines the contribution of the *Länder* to the constitutional order of the Federal Republic of Germany. This chapter presents the constitutional position of the *Länder* under the Basic Law, the significance of the *Land* constitutions, and relevant political science explanations. The fourth chapter deals with the voters in the *Länder* and works out how the "people"[1] in these *Länder* participate (or at least could participate if they wanted to). In particular, we will examine whether and to what extent representative and direct democratic procedures complement or exclude each other. The fifth chapter deals with parties and

---

[1] In recent years, the German term "Volk" (people) has become—once again—highly charged politically. In this charged version, "Volk" is a political community composed of ethnically homogeneous members. Such an understanding is sociologically, theoretically and constitutionally meaningless. In a pluralistic society, free self-determination can only be effectively and democratically expressed if and only if social heterogeneity and diversity are recognized.

examines the tasks and development of parties and party systems in the 16 *Länder*. The sixth chapter presents the constitutional organs in the *Länder* and asks how the division of powers at this level of government works. The chapter describes the importance of *Land* parliaments, examines *Land* governments and analyses the role of *Land* constitutional courts. The seventh chapter deals with mechanisms of unification, the Bundesrat (Federal Council), and the importance of the European Union for the German *Länder*. Finally, the eighth chapter concludes by discussing the contribution of the *Länder* to democracy in Germany.

The present account follows on from studies I have conducted over the last two decades (e.g. Reutter, 2008, 2018a, b; Reutter, 2012; Leunig & Reutter, 2012). In the following, I will repeatedly refer to these and other studies I have published; in part, I will adopt the considerations made there or adjust them in a more or less modified way.

This volume of the Elements of Politics textbook series is designed to introduce students of political science, social science, law, and the humanities in particular to the fundamentals of politics in the *Länder*. The format of the textbook series requires that a topic be treated as concisely as it is self-contained. Consequently, the presentation must focus on the essentials, that is, on what constitutes the substantive core of each chapter. This makes typifying generalizations a must. Such typification, however, contrasts with a basic message of the textbook: namely, the diversity of *Länder*. I have tried to meet both requirements.

A final remark on terminology: The Basic Law knows only *Land* or *Länder*, not federal states (*Bundesländer*). Thus, the second section of the Basic Law is entitled "The Federation and the *Länder*", and the *Bundesrat* consists of the governments of the *Länder* (Article 51 (1) of the Basic Law). Other examples could easily be given. This suggests that *Länder* are not "of" the Federation, but consist of their own right, as the former Minister President of Thuringia Dieter Althaus apparently liked to emphasize (Leunig, 2012, p. 19). In the following, however, I will use both terms as well as the term "constituent state", which also does not occur in the Basic Law, but can be found in some *Land* constitutions (for example, in the constitution of Baden-Wurttemberg or of Bavaria).

The *Länder*: How they Became what they are

2

Abstract

There were *Länder* before the Federal Republic of Germany (FRG) and the German Democratic Republic (GDR) came into being. The second chapter provides an overview of the creation of the *Länder,* and their contribution to the founding of the two German states in 1949, as well as to the drafting and adoption of the Basic Law and the Constitution of the German Democratic Republic, respectively. It also presents: the creation of the *Land* of Baden-Württemberg, the accession of the Saarland to the Federal Republic of Germany, the failed merger of Berlin and Brandenburg, and the accession of the five new *Länder* to the scope of the Basic Law. Finally, socio-economic and cultural differences between the *Länder* are examined.

2.1 Prehistory: The *Länder* Between the End and Beginning

The minister presidents of the 13 *Flächenländer* (area states), the first mayor and president of the Senate of the Free and Hanseatic City of Hamburg, the governing mayor of Berlin and the first mayor and president of the Senate of the Free Hanseatic City of Bremen—or in short: the heads of government of the 16 *Länder*—like to emphasize that it was they who founded the Federal Republic of Germany. Well, not them exactly as persons, of course, but the territorial authorities, i.e. the *Länder*, they represent. And they are right to emphasize this. Because before the Federal Republic of Germany there were *Länder*. It was the representatives of the *Länder*—the minister presidents and mayors of the time—who were "authorized" by the military governors of the American, British and French occupation zones in July 1948 to convene a "Constituent Assembly". In this assembly, a "democratic constitution" was to be worked out in order to "establish for the participating states a governmental structure of federal type which is best adapted to the eventual re-establishment of German unity at present disrupted, and which sill protect the rights of the participating states, provide adequate authority, and contain guarantees of individual rights and freedoms". This was the mandate given by the military governors of the three Western occupation zones to the prime ministers of the eleven West German *Länder* existing at the time (Berlin had a special status).

The mandate was contained in the "Frankfurt Documents" which were handed out to the minister presidents on July 1, 1948 (Parlamentarischer Rat, Vol. 1, 1975, p. 31)[1] A government structure "of the federal type" was supposed to suit best to restore the "presently torn German unity", while at the same time "protecting the rights of the participating states" and "creating an appropriate central authority". This, at least, was the opinion of the military governors of the Western occupation zone as well as Belgium, the Netherlands and Luxembourg, who had decided in the so-called London Six-Power Conference in 1948 to establish a Western state. Such a constitution would have to create an appropriate central authority and guarantee the individual rights and freedoms of its citizens. The minister presidents of the *Flächenländer* (area states) and the mayors of the city-states of Hamburg and Bremen fulfilled this mandate—but not without making some important changes. And it should not be forgotten that five *Länder* with constitutions also existed in the Soviet occupation zone, which was to become the German Democratic Republic in 1949. This historical starting position—some also inaccurately call it "zero hour"—continues to shape the self-image of the German *Länder* in the Federal Republic of Germany to this day.

Fascism and the Second World War had left the German Reich, which according to the ideas of the National Socialists should have lasted a thousand years, destroyed after twelve years. Militarily, the Third Reich had been defeated long before the unconditional surrender on May 8, 1945. Consequently, this surrender, which was declared once in Reims and another time in Berlin-Karlshorst, did not admit defeat, but sealed the end of the Third Reich and ushered in liberation from fascism. What fascism and war had left was a "Zusammenbruchgesellschaft", a collapsed society (Kleßmann, 1991, pp. 37–65). This was also and especially true for the political order and political institutions.

There were no *Länder* in the Third Reich. After the handover of power to Hitler on January 30, 1933 by the old elites of the Weimar Republic, the constitutional orders of the then existing 17 *Länder* had first been suspended by the appointment of *Reichsstatthalter* (Governors of the Reich). A transformation of the *Länder* took place after the elections to the Reichstag of March 5, 1933 by the laws of March 31, 1933 and April 7, 1933. With the law on the reconstruction of the Reich of January

---

[1]The German Bundestag, together with the Federal Archives, has published all the files and minutes produced before and during the deliberations in the Parliamentary Council (Parlamentarischer Rat 1975 ff.). The edition comprises 14 volumes published from 1975 onwards; the last volume was published in 2009. I took the english quotes from Ruhm von Oppen 1955, pp. 315/316.

Table 2.1 Chronological table on the founding of the Federal Republic of Germany and the German Democratic Republic (Berlin is a special case). (*Sources* Own compilation based on Kleßmann, 1991, pp. 535–540; Benz, W., 1994, pp. 258–266)

Event	American occupation zone	British occupation zone	French occupation zone	Soviet occupation zone
Surrender	May 07/08, 1945: Unconditional surrender in Reims and Berlin-Karlshorst			
Establishment of the Länder	Sept. 1945 (BAV, HES, BRE [from Jan. 1947; Jan./ Feb. 1947] Wrttbg.-Baden)	August 1946 (NRW, LS; SH, HAM [May 1946], ªBRE [until Dec. 1946])	August 1946 (RP, Baden, Wrttbg.- Hohenzollern; [special status for SLD])	ᵇJuly 1945 (MW, SAY, TH, BB, SAT)
Zonal management	October 1945 Council of Länder	From March 1946 Zone Advisory Council	From 1948 Secretariat of the Ministerial Conferences	From July 1945: German central administrations
First Land elections	Nov. 24/Dec. 1, 1946	April 20, 1947	May 18, 1947	Oct. 20, 1946
Land constitutions and constitutional referenda	1946/1947	1950–1952	1947	1946/1947
Supra-zonal cooperation	As of Jan. 1, 1947 (Bizone)		–	–
	June 20, 1948 (from April 1, 1949: "Trizone")			June 24, 1948
Origin of the Basic Law/ Constitution of the GDR	July 1, 1948: Handing over of the Frankfurt documents			
	Aug. 10–23, 1948: Convention of Herrenchiemsee			March 19, 1949: Approval by People's Council; Oct. 7, 1949: Entry into force
	Sept. 1, 1948–May 23, 1949: Parliamentary Council			

ªBremen was annexed to the American occupation zone in December 1946
ᵇThe five existing *Länder* of the Soviet zone were transformed into districts in 1952

30, 1934, the *Länder* were brought into line and made subject to the Führer principle. The *Länder* were then, according to Sven Leunig (2012, p. 25) accurately, a "mere torso in the status of administrative bodies". The war economy and the consequences of war also destroyed this torso. In May 1945, the Allies were therefore unable to fall back on any functioning political or administrative structures, although they did partially connect to existing administrative boundary lines. Moreover, they were also unable to agree on a uniform occupation policy towards Germany (Glaeßner, 2006, pp. 31–34; Benz, W., 1989, pp. 11–34; Hrbek, 2019). At least there was agreement in two respects: Prussia was to be dissolved as a stronghold of militarism and authoritarianism; furthermore, it was to be made impossible for Germany to start another war. But this minimal consensus could only be partially translated into practical policy. Developments differed in the four occupation zones after the unconditional surrender (Table 2.1). Only in retrospect can parallels be discerned.

For the *Länder*, this had a double consequence: on the one hand, the currently existing *Länder*—apart from a few exceptions—cannot look back on any historical predecessors. They are "largely creations of art" (Sturm, 2015, p. 74; Weichlein, 2019, p. 18). They emerged after 1945, as a result of military and occupation policy considerations. Nevertheless, they quickly developed inertia after their establishment. Apart from Baden-Württemberg, they still exist today more or less in the borders they had already possessed in 1949, when the Federal Republic of Germany and the German Democratic Republic were founded, respectively. On the other hand, the Western *Länder*, which were established in 1945/1946 benefited from the central guiding principle of Western occupation policy, namely to build up the German order of rule to be established "from the bottom up", i.e. from the municipalities via the districts to the *Länder* (Laufer & Münch, 2010, p. 68; Hrbek, 2019). This provided the *Länder* a formative role in the establishment of the Federal Republic of Germany. This was different in the Soviet Occupation Zone.

The establishment of the *Länder*, their development and their successive cooperation followed a similar dramaturgy, which, however, unfolded differently in the occupation zones and seems to follow an internal logic only in retrospect (see further Leunig, 2012, pp. 25–36; Kleßmann, 1991, pp. 66–78 and pp. 177–217; Benz, W., 1989; Glaeßner, 2006, pp. 279–299).

- *American occupation zone*: Although *Länder* were first installed in the Soviet occupation zone, the American military government under General Clay was the pioneer and pace-setter for developments after the unconditional surrender. The plan of the former American Secretary of the Treasury Henry Morgenthau Jr. to split the German Reich into agrarian regions after the end of the war, to demilitarize it and thus permanently eliminate Germany as a belligerent power, is quoted with pleasure. But it was never seriously considered by the American government of the time under Franklin D. Roosevelt. It quickly disappeared into an earthen drawer and was, according to Wolfgang Benz (1994, p. 38), no more than an "episode"; today it serves mainly as a "legend" to fuel anti-American resentment (ibid.). The U.S. sought a rapid reestablishment of *Länder* and a bottom-up construction of democracy. Therefore, only a few months after the unconditional surrender, the American military government created the *Länder*: Bavaria, Württemberg-Baden, and (Greater) Hesse and appointed minister presidents (Leunig, 2012, pp. 27–30). As early as October 1945, a *Länder* Council was created to coordinate administrative matters between the *Länder* (Kleßmann, 1991, pp. 76–78). In June 1946, elections to constituent assemblies were held in the *Länder* of the American occupation zone, and in November and December of the same year, *Landtag* elections and referendums on constitutions were held. This created the conditions for democratic self-determination. Thereafter, according to Sven Leunig (2012, p. 29), the Americans withdrew from operational politics and administration and "henceforth enforced their policies less by command than by observation and consultation."

- British *occupation zone*: Developments in the British occupation zone took place with a time lag and in a somewhat different sequence but led to similar results. In March 1946, for example, the British Military Government set up a Zonal Advisory Council which had an advisory function. The *Länder* of Schleswig–Holstein, North Rhine-Westphalia and Lower Saxony were not established until afterwards, in July and August 1946 respectively, almost a year later than the *Länder* in the American occupation zone. Hamburg and Bremen, which was ceded to the American military government in December 1946, were declared city-states in May 1946. Consequently, *Land* elections and the adoption of *Land* constitutions took place later in the British occupation zone than in the *Länder* in the American occupation zone. As a result, the bloc confrontation that intensified from March 1947 onwards and the Basic Law that came into force from May 23 to 24, 1949 developed a formative force on developments in these *Länder*. It is also important to note that with the creation of the *Länder* in 1946, governments could also be democratically legitimized in the British occupation zone, and that supra-zonal cooperation became possible from 1947. The Bizone, created on January 1, 1947, in which the *Länder* of the British and American occupation zones were united, was to develop into the precursor of the Federal Republic of Germany.
- *French occupation zone*: *the* establishment of *Länder* in the American and British occupation zones, *Land* elections, constitutional assemblies in the *Länder* of the American occupation zone, the establishment of the Bizone and the East–West conflict that had been intensifying since 1947—all these factors unfolded a dynamic that even the French military government could not escape. The French military government only "reluctantly settled for a common Western approach" (Glaeßner, 2006, p. 284) and originally aimed to "divide Germany into as many, small, largely sovereign, and at best state-aligned *Länder* as possible" (Leunig, 2012, p. 33). This was understandable as France had been invaded twice by Germany within a quarter of a century. France therefore wanted a confederation of states in which the German *Länder* would only be loosely connected. In August 1946, the French military government created the *Länder* of Rhineland-Palatinate, Baden, and Württemberg-Hohenzollern; the Saar region had a special status. In May 1947, the French military government had *Land* parliaments elected and *Land* constitutions adopted. The *Länder* in the French Zone occupation zone were not encouraged to coordinate their policies. Moreover, the Saarland was placed directly under the French administration and tutelage.
- *Soviet occupation zone*: Curiously, the SMAD, the Soviet Military Administration, was the first occupying power to create *Länder* in the zone it occupied in July 1945 (Leunig, 2012, pp. 34–36; Kleßmann, 1991, pp. 66–78) and establish administrative structures. To be sure, it took until June 1946 for advisory *Land* assemblies to be set up. *Land* elections were held in October 1946, and *Land* constitutions were adopted beginning in December 1947. However, this federalist intermezzo had a rather instrumental character anyway. For the *Land* governments also remained under the control of the SMAD,

which had already established "central administrations" in 1945. The *Länder* of Thuringia, Mecklenburg-Western Pomerania and Saxony, which had been created during the occupation, as well as the province of Saxony-Anhalt and the Mark Brandenburg were dissolved again shortly after the founding of the GDR and replaced by districts. The postulate contained in Article 1 (1) of the 1949 constitution of the GDR that "Germany (sic!) is an indivisible democratic republic" and is built on the "German *Länder*" was mere lip service.

It was under these conditions that the two German states were founded. Both foundations were embedded in the bloc confrontation between West and East. It was also a question of which system would prevail: Western democracy or real existing socialism. The creation of the western state was also pre-determined by the existing *Länder*, the currency reform carried out in June 1948, the creation of the social market economy and the interests of the western allies. In other words, crucial preliminary decisions on constitutional policy had already been made before the decision was taken at the London Six-Power Conference in 1948 to instruct the Länder in the western occupation zones to give themselves an overall constitution and to establish a western state. The only contact persons for this project were the representatives legitimized by the people of the *Länder* through elections: the prime ministers and the mayors of Bremen and Hamburg (Berlin had a special role). The development in the Soviet occupation zone was different. Although there were *Länder* here as well, they did not play a major role in the founding of the GDR.

The deliberations in the Parliamentary Council (Parlamentarischer Rat), which was to draft the Basic Law, did not take place without preconditions. The ideas of the Allies, the looming division of Germany, the intensifying East–West conflict, the preliminary decisions already taken on the economic and social order and, finally, the ideas of the *Länder* shaped the deliberations in the Parliamentary Council. However, this is not a peculiarity of this constitutional convention. No constitution is created in a vacuum. Nevertheless, the Parliamentary Council represents a caesura in post-war development in two respects: On the one hand, it was the first institution with a west-zone character. Decisions were no longer taken at the Länder or zonal level, but at the supra-zonal level. On the other hand, this pushed the heads of the *Land* governments into the background. They were replaced by the parties, which determined the decision- and will-making process in the Parliamentary Council and thereafter.

The Parliamentary Council functioned as its name suggests: like a parliament with specialized committees, working bodies, and along the party affiliation of the members (Benz, W., 1989, pp. 191–235; Niclauß, 1998; Sörgel, 1985). The 65 members of the Parliamentary Council, who had been elected by the *Land* parliaments and thus reflected the majority ratios there, met for the first time on September 1, 1948, at the Pedagogical Academy in Bonn. The CDU had 19 seats (+1 from Berlin), the CSU 8, the SPD 27 (+3 from Berlin), the FDP/DVP/LDP 5 (+1 from Berlin), the German Party (Deutsche Partei), the Center Party (Zentrum) and the KPD 2 seats each. Konrad Adenauer of the CDU was elected president. (The Berlin members were not entitled to vote in the final vote). The draft Basic

Law was passed in the Parliamentary Council on May 8, 1949 by 53 votes to 12. With the exception of the Bavarian *Landtag,* all (West) German *Land* parliaments existing at the time subsequently adopted the Basic Law. The Bavarian *Landtag's* "No" to the Basic Law was, moreover, a sort of window-dressing. For the Bavarian *Landtag,* for which the Basic Law was not federalist enough, stressed in a second resolution that Bavaria would abide by the Basic Law should it be adopted by two-thirds of the *Länder* and thus enter into force.

The deliberations in the Parliamentary Council were complicated and marked by conflicts (Niclauß, 1998; Sörgel, 1985). These conflicts concerned fundamental issues of the state to be established (such as individual fundamental rights) as well as its organizational structure. The structure and distribution of competences in the federal state were even to prove highly controversial matters. The composition and competences of the *Bundesrat* (Federal Council), the legislative competences of the Federation and the *Länder*, and the financial constitution—in short, all the constitutive elements of the German federal state—were in dispute. It is therefore hardly surprising that precisely these regulations were later amended again and again.

The *Länder* played an important role in the constitutional debates. Their heads of government had not only been given the task of drafting a constitution. They had also seized the opportunity and set up a committee with representatives from eleven *Länder* beforehand. The Constitutional Convention of Herrenchiemsee, named after its meeting place, met from August 10 to 23, 1948 and drew up a preliminary draft for the Basic Law. The Convention mainly brought together legal expertise (Glaeßner, 2006, p. 292). Moreover, about 67 % of the members of the Parliamentary Council were also members of a *Land* parliament (Sörgel, 1985, p. 260; Glaeßner, 2006, p. 294). And not to be forgotten: The Basic Law had to be adopted by the *Land* parliaments.

Finally, two things should be noted: First, it is sometimes claimed that the founding of the Federal Republic of Germany was the result of an "octroi" by the Western Allies. It was carried out in the name of, by order of, and on behalf of the USA, Great Britain and France, and was not based on a free decision of the "German people". This is substantiated by the Frankfurt documents and by the fact that the Basic Law was not adopted in a referendum and had to be approved by the occupying powers. However, such a view overlooks the fact that prime ministers, Land governments and members of the Parliamentary Council were in complete agreement with the ideas of the Western Allies. They too wanted to establish a democratic federal state that had to abide by law (Niclauß, 1998; Sörgel, 1985). Moreover, they were in a position to push through their own ideas. For example, the Western Allies wanted to have the constitution adopted in a referendum, a request that the prime ministers successfully rebuffed. Nor were the Allies able to push through their wish to have the members of the "Constituent Assembly" directly elected. Here, too, the prime ministers prevailed with their proposal to have the members of the Parliamentary Council elected by the *Land* parliaments. Moreover, a "German people" that could have adopted a constitution did not exist in the sense of constitutional law anyway. It was only created with the Basic Law.

Secondly, it is repeatedly argued that the Basic Law is merely a "provisional" constitution that will be replaced by a "proper" one as soon as the two German states are reunited. This can be justified by the name (Basic Law [*Grundgesetz*] instead of Constitution), the history of its creation and some constitutional provisions that had lost their meaning in 1990 and were deleted. However, this political context does not change the fact that the Basic Law has always been understood formally and materially as a full constitution. It regulates the structure of the state, the relationship between the state and its citizens and, moreover, could and can only be amended by a qualified majority. It therefore fulfils all the conditions of a full constitution. More importantly, once it came into force, the Basic Law took effect. In case of doubt or dispute, the Federal Constitutional Court helped.

In the Soviet occupation zone, the development took a different course. The *Länder* established in 1945 played no role in the founding of the GDR and the adoption of the constitution in 1949. The founding of the German Democratic Republic and the drafting of the constitution were controlled and dominated by the SED, which had emerged from the forced unification of the SPD and the KPD. It followed Walter Ulbricht's[2] injunction that while it should "look democratic", the KPD or SED should "have everything in its hands" (quoted in Leonhard, 1966, p. 294). The chronology of events confirms this assessment: the People's Congress (*Volkskongress*) convened in the Soviet occupation zone at the end of 1947 consisted of delegates from businesses, social groups and associations (farmers, artists, scientists) who had not been elected, but rather "invited". From it emerged the "German People's Council", which drew up a draft constitution for the whole of Germany. The Third German People's Congress, elected according to unified lists, established a People's Council, which enacted the constitution of the GDR in October 1949 (Glaeßner, 2006, pp. 177–186; Kleßmann, 1991, pp. 202–208).

Berlin had a special status (the Saarland is discussed below). Berlin was jointly governed by the four occupying powers (Massing, 1990; Wettig, 1999). For this purpose, an Allied Command was established, in which all four occupying powers were equally represented and which exercised supreme governmental authority in Berlin. However, in Berlin, the conflicts between the Western occupying powers and the Soviet Union escalated into an "open power struggle" (Massing, 1990, p. 136). The Soviet Union had taken the currency reform carried out in the Western occupation zones on June 1, 1948 as an opportunity to prohibit all goods and passenger traffic to and from Berlin and had withdrawn from the Allied Command. West Berlin was thus cut off from all supplies. In consequence, the Western powers, and the USA in particular, saw the protection of Berlin—and the containment of the Soviet claim to power—as a challenge and supplied the population of West Berlin by air ("Berlin Airlift"). The Berlin Blockade, which lasted from June 24,

---

[2]Walter Ulbricht (1893–1973) returned from the Soviet Union ("Ulbricht Group") to Berlin in April 1945 and assumed leading functions in the state and party after the founding of the GDR (Leonhard, 1966, pp. 275–279).

1948 to May 12, 1949, sealed the division of the city (Wettig, 1999, pp. 160–166). West and East Berlin subsequently took different directions. While East Berlin was declared the capital of the GDR, the Western Allies ruled out a full incorporation of West Berlin into the FRG. Until 1990, Berlin remained under Allied control, had no voting members in the Bundestag (Federal Diet) and Bundesrat (Federal Council), and had to adopt all federal laws by resolution of the regional parliament, the House of Representatives.

Overall, this results in a heterogeneous picture (Table 2.2) of the history of state law. The *Länder* became part of the Federal Republic of Germany at different times and show considerable differences in size and population (Table 2.3).

Table 2.2 The German *Länder:* foundation and constitutions. (*Sources* Own compilation; Reutter, 2018b, p. 58; www.election.de)

	Date of founding[a]	Election to the first *Land* parliament	First Constitution (entry into force)[b]	"Accession" to the FRG[c]
BW[d]	04/25/1952	03/09/1952	11/20/1953	05/23/1949
BAV	09/19/1945	12/01/1946	12/08/1946	05/23/1949
BER	10/03/1990	10/20/1946	10/01/1950	10/03/1990
BB	10/03/1990	10/14/1990	08/21/1992	10/03/1990
BRE	01/23/1947	10/12/1947	10/22/1947	05/23/1949
HAM	05/15/1945	10/13/1946	07/01/1952	05/23/1949
HES	09/19/1945	12/01/1946	12/01/1946	05/23/1949
MW	10/03/1990	10/14/1990	05/23/1993	10/03/1990
LS	11/01/1946	04/20/1947	05/01/1951	05/23/1949
NRW	07/17/1946	04/20/1947	07/11/1950	05/23/1949
RP	08/30/1946	05/18/1947	05/18/1947	05/23/1949
SLD	02/16/1946[e]	10/05/1947	12/17/1947	01/01/1957
SAY	10/03/1990	10/14/1990	06/06/1992	10/03/1990
SAT	10/03/1990	10/14/1990	07/18/1992	10/03/1990
SH	08/23/1946	04/20/1947	01/12/1950	05/23/1949
TH	10/03/1990	10/14/1990	10/16/1994	10/03/1990

[a]Date of founding: date of proclamation by military government, by appointment of a prime minister or mayor (HH); in the case of BB, MW, SAY, SAT and TH, date of refounding
[b]For BB, MW, SAN, SAT and TH entry into force of the constitution adopted after unification
[c]Date of founding of the Federal Republic of Germany, in the case of Saarland and the new Länder: date of accession of the Land or the GDR
[d]Baden, Württemberg-Baden and Württemberg-Hohenzollern, which merged to Baden-Württemberg in 1952, had been part of the Federal Republic of Germany since May 23, 1949
[e]Saarland came under French control on 16 February 1946 and joined the FRG on January 1, 1957

Table 2.3 *Länder:* names, capitals, areas, population (as of 12/2017). (*Source* Own compilation; Statistisches Bundesamt, 2019d, p. 26)

Land (official name)	Abbreviation	Capital	Area (km²)	Population (in thousands)	Population/km²
Land of Baden-Württemberg	BW	Stuttgart	35,748	11,023	308
Free State of Bavaria	BAV	Munich	70,542	12,997	184
Land of Berlin	BER	Berlin	891	3,613	4055
Land of Brandenburg	BB	Potsdam	29,654	2,504	84
Free Hanseatic City of Bremen	BRE	Bremen (factual)	419	681	1624
Free and Hanseatic City of Hamburg	HAM	Hamburg	755	1,831	2424
Land of Hesse	HES	Wiesbaden	21,116	6,243	294
Land of Mecklenburg-Western Pomerania	MW	Schwerin	23,294	1,611	69
Land of Lower Saxony	LS	Hanover	47,710	7,963	167
Land North Rhine-Westphalia	NRW	Düsseldorf	34,112	17,912	525
Land of Rhineland-Palatinate	RP	Mainz	19,858	4,074	205
Saarland	SLD	Saarbrücken	2,571	994	387
Free State of Saxony	SAY	Dresden	18,450	4,081	221
Land of Saxony-Anhalt	SAT	Magdeburg	20,454	2,223	109
Land of Schleswig–Holstein	SH	Kiel	15,804	2,890	183
Free State of Thuringia	TH	Erfurt	16,202	2,151	133

2.2   *Land* Borders: Reorganization, Mergers, Accessions and German Unification

As mentioned, the *Länder* are "constructs of art" (Sturm, 2015, p. 74). Their borders are the result of occupation policy and military considerations and only in a few cases correspond to historical traditions. And they exhibit serious differences in size and population strength (Table 2.3). In the second Frankfurt document, the Western occupying powers had therefore asked the prime ministers "to examine the boundaries of the several states in order to determine what modifications they want to propose. Such modifications should take account of traditional patterns, and avoid, to the extent feasible, the creation of states which are either too large or too small in comparison with other states" (Frankfurt Document II, in Ruhm von Oppen 1955, p. 316). All this should have taken place before the Constituent Assembly, which became the Parliamentary Council, was convened.

The prime ministers rejected this request. They simply considered it impossible to carry out the desired territorial reform in the short time until the convening of the Parliamentary Council. The military governors accepted the concerns. Since then, the demand for a reorganization of the federal territory has been on the political agenda—but very low down. Every now and then it moved up a few places, and at times it was even seriously considered, such as in the Ernst Commission in the mid-1970s, or as after German unification in 1990, but never really tackled (Schwarz, 2012). Again and again the same thing is called for: the creation of *Länder* of roughly equal size and strength. After all, the borders drawn by the Allies would have created Länder that would not be able to fulfil their tasks and would have to rely on support from the federal government or from other *Länder* (Kropp, 2010, p. 132). But so far the reservations have been too great and the territorial insistence too strong. Perhaps, however, the arguments are not good enough.

However, this does not mean that the territorial structure of the German federal state has remained unchanged. On the contrary, there was a merger, the accession of the Saarland in 1957, the creation and integration of five new *Länder,* the formation of the *Land* of Berlin, and the failed merger of Berlin and Brandenburg in 1995/96. I will spare myself an overview of the various attempts, commissions, and plans that were presented time and again and all came to nothing (Schwarz, 2012, Sturm, 2001, pp. 91–100), and limit the presentation to the three major territorial changes in the history of the German federal state. I am referring to the successful merger of Baden, Württemberg-Hohenzollern, and Württemberg-Baden in 1952, the accession of Saarland to the Federal Republic of Germany in 1957, and the accession of the five East German *Länder* to the scope of the Basic Law in 1990 in the course of German unification. In addition, I will discuss the failed merger of Berlin and Brandenburg in 1996.

Baden-Württemberg: The merger of the three south-western *Länder* of Baden, Württemberg-Baden and Württemberg-Hohenzollern to form the present *Land* Baden-Württemberg was a kind of "Swabian prank" at the expense of (southern) Badeners. Constitutionally, the merger was not carried out on the basis of Article

29 of the Basic Law, which in eight paragraphs provided for a complicated and impractical procedure for such cases. The then minister-president of Württemberg-Hohenzollern had already proposed to the Parliamentary Council that a simplified procedure be provided for the south-western *Land* to be founded (Schneider, 1990, p. 55). According to the subsequently inserted Article 118 of the Basic Law, the merger of the three participating *Länder* was to take place either by "agreement" or on the basis of a federal law, which, however, had to provide for a referendum. Since it quickly became clear that the (South) Baden government under Leo Wohleb would reject a merger and that an "agreement" was thus impossible, the governments of Württemberg-Baden and Württemberg-Hohenzollern sought the second procedure, i.e. merger by federal law and referendum. The law passed created four voting districts, and the merger of the three states was to take place if a majority in three of the four voting districts voted for the south-western *Land*. This is exactly what happened. While a majority in South Baden voted against the merger in the referendum on December 9, 1951, a majority in North Baden, North Württemberg, and South Württemberg voted in favor (Schneider, 1990, p. 56). A constitutional assembly was elected in March 1952, and the first minister-president was sworn in in April 1952. The *Land* of Baden-Württemberg had thus come into being, but the very last word had not yet been spoken. For the people of Baden had successfully carried out another referendum in the autumn of 1956 on the basis of Article 29 of the Basic Law. However, the necessary referendum was postponed again and again. It did not take place until many years later and only after the Federal Constitutional Court had issued a ruling to this effect. The referendum finally scheduled for June 7, 1970 was held only in the Baden part of the *Land* and confirmed the normative force of the factual. What was and had proven itself was to remain. Nearly 82 % of those voting voted for Baden to remain in the *Land* of Baden-Württemberg (Wehling, 2004a, pp. 21–26; Schneider, 1990, pp. 54–56; Sturm, 2001, pp. 92–93).

Berlin-Brandenburg: A second attempt to merge *Länder* took place after German unification, which had put the debate about a reorganization of the federal territory once again on the political agenda—and once again without consequences. The *Land* of Berlin, created in 1990, and the *Land* of Brandenburg, re-established in the same year, wanted to do their part and create the hyphenated *Land* of "Berlin-Brandenburg" in 1995 (Jung, 1997; Lorenz, 2016). As in the case of Baden-Württemberg, Article 29 of the Basic Law, which was intended for such cases, was not invoked for this purpose. Rather, the Basic Law was amended in 1994 and an exception was created with Article 118a of the Basic Law. According to this, the "reorganization of Berlin and Brandenburg" could be made possible by agreement between the two Länder—but only "with the participation of their inhabitants who are entitled to vote" (Art. 118a of the Basic Law). This last condition was to prove an insurmountable hurdle. It is true that the then *Land* governments of Berlin and Brandenburg concluded a so-called merger agreement, which was also adopted by both *Land* parliaments with the necessary two-thirds majority (only the then PDS voted against it). But the merger failed because of the vote of the voters of Brandenburg. In Berlin, 53.4 % voted for the merger in

the referendum on May 5, 1996 (with a voter turnout of 57.8 %), but the project
in Brandenburg already failed because only 36.6 % of those voting supported the
merger (with a voter turnout of 66.4 %; Jung 1997). Since then, there has been no
renewed attempt to merge these two *Länder*—or any other *Länder* for that matter.
The reorganization of the federal territory was and is more of a pipe dream than a
realistic option.

Saarland: The Basic Law offered yet another possibility for changing the
territorial structure of the federal state: accession on the basis of the now abolished Article 23 of the Basic Law. The Saarland and later the five new *Länder*
of the GDR became part of the Federal Republic of Germany via this route. The
Saarland had already been carved out of the French occupation zone in 1946
(Leunig, 2012, pp. 41 f.; Plöhn & Barz, 1990, pp. 384–386; Rütters, 2012, pp.
471–474). It was a French "protectorate" (Plöhn & Barz, 1990, p. 385). This "protectorate" had its own currency, had given itself a constitution in 1947, and its
inhabitants even had their own citizenship. Nevertheless, the status of the Saarland
was "unresolved" (Plöhn & Barz, 1990, p. 385). The Western integration sought
by the then Chancellor Konrad Adenauer (CDU) made it possible to conclude
an agreement with France. The agreed Saar Statute stipulated that the Saarland
would remain economically linked to France, but that it would be represented
externally by a commissioner of the Western European Union that never came
into being. However, in a referendum on October 23, 1955, 67.7 % of those voting—the turnout was 96.6 %—voted against this statute and thus in favour of the
Saarland's annexation to the Federal Republic of Germany. As a result, the incumbent Saarland government resigned, the *Land* parliament applied for the necessary
accession to the Federal Republic of Germany in accordance with Article 23 of the
Basic Law, and the *Bundestag* (Federal Diet) passed the necessary incorporation
law. The Saarland thus joined the scope of the Basic Law and the Federal Republic
of Germany on January 1, 1957.

Unification: The incorporation of the five East German or, in other words,
German unification, was also carried out on the basis of Article 23 of the Basic
Law (Glaeßner, 2006, pp. 334–347). Yet, the incorporation of the five East German
Länder into the Federal Republic of Germany was managed in a completely
different manner than the accession of the Saarland. Originally, it was envisaged that the unification of the two German states would take place in accordance with the then applicable Article 146 of the German constitution. According
to this article, the Federal Republic of Germany would have been reconstituted
and the "German people" would have given themselves a new constitution in a
"free decision". As is well known, things turned out differently. The new constitution did not take place, nor did the "free decision" of the "German people".
Instead, the "quick and uncomplicated way of the GDR's accession to the Federal
Republic" was chosen (Glaeßner, 2006, p. 335). This accession took place on
the basis of the "State Treaty on Monetary, Economic and Social Union" and the
"Unification Treaty" between the two German states on October 3, 1990. Article
1 of the Unification Treaty of August 31, 1990 stipulated: "With the coming
into effect of the accession of the German Democratic Republic to the Federal

Republic of Germany in accordance with Article 23 of the Basic Law on 3 October 1990, the Länder of Brandenburg, Mecklenburg-Western Pomerania, Saxony, Saxony-Anhalt and Thuringia shall become Länder of the Federal Republic of Germany. The formation and boundaries of these states among themselves shall be governed by the provisions of the Constitutional Law on the Formation of Länder in the German Democratic Republic of July 22, 1990." And further: "The 23 districts of Berlin form the Land of Berlin." On October 14, 1990, all five East German *Länder* elected their *Landtag* (state parliaments), and on December 2, 1990, Berlin elected its first all-Berlin House of Representatives (Abgeordnetenhaus). All the *Länder* that were created in 1990 eventually gave themselves a new constitution; Berlin fundamentally revised its constitution and put the new basic order into effect by referendum in 1995.

The number of the *Länder* and the territorial structure of the federal territory are thus the result of three factors: the foundings by the Allies, one successful and one failed merger, and the accession of the Saarland and the GDR to the scope of the Basic Law. The accessions were made possible by the now abolished Article 23 of the Basic Law. In its version adopted in 1949, it reads as follows: "This Basic Law shall initially apply in the territories of the Länder of Baden, Bavaria, Bremen, Greater Berlin, Hamburg, Hesse, Lower Saxony, North Rhine-Westphalia, Rhineland-Palatinate, Schleswig–Holstein, Württemberg-Baden and Württemberg-Hohenzollern. In other parts of Germany, it will have to come into force after their accession." This article was repealed in 1990 by the Unification Treaty and replaced in 1992 by stipulations on the European Union. If one disregards the fact that in Article 23 until 1990 the Länder "Baden", "Groß-Berlin", "Württemberg-Baden" and "Württemberg-Hohenzollern" were named and Saarland was missing, this basis created a flexible possibility to join the scope of the Basic Law. A vote was just as little necessary for this in the FRG as a general revision of the Basic Law. The accession of the Saarland and the accession of the GDR to the area of application of the Basic Law were able to take place comparatively smoothly from a constitutional perspective. The federal state thus demonstrated flexibility and gained in diversity—or heterogeneity.

2.3   Equivalent Living Conditions, Unitarism and Differences: Society, Economy and Culture in the *Länder*

The counterpart to the principle of federal diversity is the guiding principle of the "equivalence of living conditions", which is rather associated with unitary states (Kropp, 2010, p. 15 f.). However, according to Hartmut Klatt, federalism is accepted in Germany (only) on the condition that politics "orders living conditions as uniformly as in a central state" (Klatt, 2004, p. 10). Surveys confirm this assumption (Bertelsmann Stiftung, 2008, p. 18; Petersen et al., 2008). In the relevant literature, the conclusion formulated by Konrad Hesse (1962) that we live in a "unitary federal state" is shared. Such a state is characterized by the fact that although it is structured like a federal state, it functions like a unitary state. All important decisions are made at the federal level: moreover, the *Länder* are denied any "individuality". In this perspective, the constitutional mandate to create "equal" living conditions[3] has led to the levelling of all relevant differences between the *Länder*. The Federal Republic of Germany is thus in reality a "disguised unitary state" (Abromeit, 1992).

Now, even in "non-disguised" unitary states such as France and Great Britain, living conditions are by no means equivalent or even uniform everywhere. Life in Paris is undoubtedly different from life in the French provinces, and the prosperous south-east of England can hardly be compared with the de-industrialised regions of the English Midlands. For this reason alone, it would be unrealistic to assume that the same living conditions exist everywhere in Germany. And quite logically, the German government set up the "Equivalent Living Conditions" Commission in July 2018. The commission's mission was to investigate "an equitable distribution of resources and opportunities" and to develop proposals to "achieve equivalence" (BMI, 2019, p. 8). For the Commission, the term "equivalent living conditions" means "good development opportunities and fair participation opportunities for all people living in Germany" (ibid.). In its final report, the Commission also discovered a "considerable need for action". It thus seems more than appropriate to set out some differences between the states.

It should be noted at the outset, however, that it is difficult to determine what is meant by the term "equivalent living conditions". The above-mentioned paraphrase of the Government Commission as "good development opportunities and fair participation opportunities for all people living in Germany" (BMI, 2019, p. 8) does not lead much further. Moreover, Ragnitz and Thum (2019, p. 14) rightly point out that there is no consensus on "which indicators should be used to measure living conditions". Similarly, it is unclear how the indicators should be weighted or which spatial reference level (region, country, etc.) should be chosen. Even more important is the problem of how to assess differences. In most cases, a statistically determined national average is used as a benchmark in relevant studies. A below-average endowment in one area is then interpreted as a violation of "equivalence" (Ragnitz & Thum, 2019, p. 13 f.). Behind the concept of equivalence, however, lies a normative idea about a just society, which can hardly be expressed in statistical terms. In the following, therefore I only highlight a few selected differences between *Länder*. The questions of how these differences are to be evaluated or whether they represent a violation of the principle of equivalence of living conditions will not be addressed.

First, let's look at demographic developments (see Table 2.4). They point to an east–west difference (Krumm, 2015, pp. 192–195; Statistisches Bundesamt, 2019c, pp. 23–84). For example, the eastern German *Länder* experienced a steady population decline after 1990. They showed a negative net migration until 2017,

---

[3]Until 1994, the Basic Law even demanded "uniform living conditions".

Table 2.4 Länder profiles: society, economy and culture. (*Source* Statistisches Bundesamt, 2019a, 2019b, 2019c, 2019d, pp. 237 and 377; Arbeitskreis „Volkswirtschaftliche Gesamtrechnungen der Länder", 2019; Statistische Ämter der Länder, 2019; Faus et al., 2019, p. 51)

(Year)	Foreigners (in %)	Manufacturing industry[a]	Unemployment rate (%)	GDP/ Inhabitant (abs.)	Income/ Inhabitant	Satisfied Democrats	Catholics	Protestants	Muslims	Other religions, non-denominational	Debt/ Inhabitants[b]	Minimum protection rate[c]
	(2018)	(2018)	(2018)	(2017)	(2017)	(2018)	(2011)	(2011)	(2011)	(2011)	(2019)	(2017)
BW	16.0	40	3.2	45,064	24,552	57.5	37	33	6	24	4,657	6
BAV	14.2	34	2.9	46,698	24,963	52.3	55	21	4	20	1,994	5
BER	21.8	15	8.1	38,864	20,330	53.8	9	19	8	63	14,876	18
BB	4.9	27	6.3	28,473	20,225	36.7	3	17	–	80	7,139	9
BRE	19.2	29	9.8	48,586	21,384	52.1	12	41	10	36	35,138	18
HAM	16.9	18	6.3	63,927	24,404	61.9	10	30	8	52	17,789	13
HES	17.4	26	4.6	45,107	23,092	56.7	25	40	7	29	8,388	9
MW	4.8	23	7.9	27,160	19,190	47.8	3	18	–	79	5,844	11
LS	10.2	33	5.3	36,178	21,920	57.8	18	50	3	30	9,328	9
NRW	14.8	28	6.8	38,276	22,263	53.7	42	28	8	23	12,565	12
RP	11.8	35	4.4	35,316	22,731	60.5	45	31	4	20	10,664	7
SLD	12.4	34	6.1	35,710	20,527	57.4	63	19	3	14	17,734	11
SAY	5.1	32	6.0	29,960	19,920	31.4	4	21	–	75	1,010	9
SAT	5.1	33	7.7	27,651	19,537	38.9	4	14	–	81	10,817	12
SH	8.8	25	5.5	32,404	22,864	57.6	6	53	3	38	11,921	10
TH	5.1	35	5.5	28,855	19,738	36.1	8	24	–	68	7,916	8

[a]Share in gross value added at current prices in %

[b]Debt of the Länder and municipalities/municipal associations per inhabitant; status: June 30, 2019

[c]Minimum income rate = the share of recipients of minimum income benefits in the total population (social assistance, basic benefits for job-seekers, etc.)

mainly because more people moved out of these *Länder* than moved in. This trend has weakened over time and even reversed for the first time in 2017. However, significantly fewer people lived in eastern German *Länder* than in 1991. With the exception of Saarland and Bremen, the number of inhabitants increased in the other *Länder*. The population increases are also due to the influx of people from abroad, which, incidentally, is also likely to be the cause of the 2017 trend reversal in the eastern German *Länder*. In any case, the share of the foreign population in all eastern German *Länder* rose from around 2 % in 2000 to around 5 % at the end of 2018. According to the Federal Statistical Office (Statistisches Bundesamt, 2019b), the eastern German *Länder* are thus still far below the national average of 13.1 %. In addition, it is mainly the urban centers (Leipzig, Halle, etc.) that have benefited from the increases. Such demographic developments have far-reaching consequences. They are reflected in the fiscal equalization, may entail municipal and administrative reforms or influence local infrastructure (Krumm, 2015, p. 192).

However, it is not only demographic trends that vary between the *Länder*, but also the economic strength and thus the prosperity of the inhabitants (Statistisches Bundesamt, 2019d, pp. 175–194 and pp. 330–354; Arbeitskreis "Volkswirtschaftliche Gesamtrechnung der Länder", 2019; Statistische Ämter der Länder, 2019). The most common indicator for measuring the economic strength of local authorities is gross domestic product (GDP) per capita. GDP captures all goods and services produced in an economy. It is a measure that only inaccurately measures economic strength. This is especially true for the *Länder* because their economies are highly interdependent across *Land* borders. But for lack of a better alternative, it can at least be determined on this basis that GDP per capita is highest in Hamburg and lowest in the eastern German states. In 2017, it was just under 64,000 euros in Hamburg, more than twice as high as in the five eastern German *Länder*. This corresponds to the fact that the unemployment rate in the southern German *Länder* is comparatively low and in the eastern German *Länder*, at an average of 6.8 %, is around 2 %age points above the national average.

These differences are reflected in income. Here, Bavaria leads the way, where each resident had an average of just under €25,000 at their disposal in 2017, around 10 % more than the national average. By contrast, residents in the five eastern German *Länder* had incomes at least 20 % points below the Bavarian top figure and at least 10 % points below the national average. The differences in economic structure are also astonishing. The share of the manufacturing sector—such as mechanical engineering, the chemical industry, and the automotive industry—is 40 % in Baden-Württemberg and only 15 and 18 % respectively in the city-states of Berlin and Hamburg. In contrast, the service sector is particularly large in these city-states.

In addition to socio-economic and demographic differences, cultural differences can also be observed. The Federal Republic of Germany is considered a secular country in which religion is a private matter and the state is neutral. Of course, these principles also apply in the *Länder*. Nevertheless, religion and the culture associated with it exert a noticeable influence on public life and politics.

Again, the differences are unsurprising, but quite astonishing in their extent (Statistisches Bundesamt, 2019c). The proportion of Catholics in the *Länder* ranges from 3 to 63 %, and for Protestants from 14 to 53 %; in the western German Länder the proportion of Muslims varies from 3 to 10 % (no data are available for the eastern German Länder).

It is sometimes said of the Weimar Republic that it was a democracy without democrats. And that is precisely what destroyed it. Against this background, a study published in 2019 by the Bertelsmann Stiftung gives cause for concern (Faus et al., 2019). For it comes to the following findings, among others: Although a majority of respondents in 2018 still considered democracy to be the best form of government, the trend was downward and had declined by seven percentage points compared to the previous year (from 76 to 69 %). The proportion of "satisfied democrats" who have a positive view of democracy as a form of government and as a lived practice has fallen from 53 (2017) to 46 % (2018) of respondents. Finally, the acceptance of democracy as a form of government was lower in the eastern *Länder* than in the western ones. Satisfied democrats are in the minority in all eastern German *Länder*. In Saxony even less than a third of respondents can be classified as satisfied democrats (Faus et al., 2019, p. 7 f. and passim).

The picture is completely different when looking at public debt and the minimum security ratio. In this area, the eastern German *Länder* perform better than average. In any case, the per capita debt of these *Länder*, municipalities and districts was well below the national average, while the share of recipients of social assistance, basic security for the unemployed, etc. was between 9 and 12 %. In Hamburg and Bremen, the debt per inhabitant in 2019 was €14,876 and €35,138 respectively. At the same time, almost one in five people in Bremen received social assistance or were dependent on basic benefits (Statistisches Bundesamt, 2019d, p. 237).

The demographic, economic and cultural differences underline the federal diversity and point out that it is by no means possible to speak of equal living conditions without further ado.

Federalism and *Länder*: Basic Constitutional Principles and Theories

3

Abstract

In the third chapter of the textbook, the two constitutional levels in the German federal state are examined and theories on German federalism are presented. The following questions are addressed: What are the fundamental constitutional principles for the structure and functioning of the federal state? Are Land constitutions constitutions at all and why do they differ? How do political science approaches explain the functioning and performance of the federal state and what role is assigned to the *Länder* in these theories?

3.1 Basic Law, the *Länder,* and German Federalism

The term federalism has its origin in the Latin word *foedus,* which denotes a federation, an alliance or a treaty. In the cooperative federalism of the Federal Republic of Germany, this idea still appears. After all, the German federal state is an organizing principle for a polity "in which fundamentally equal and independent members are united into an overarching political whole" (Laufer & Münch, 2010, p. 16). It goes without saying that a *foedus* composed of 16 equal and autonomous members cannot always function smoothly. The complicated regulations in the Basic Law and in the *Land* constitutions prove this.

"The Federal Republic of Germany is a democratic and social federal state." So says Article 20 (1) of the Basic Law. Thus, the federal state is a constitutional principle, and all important questions about the functioning of the federal state should find answers in the German Federal Constitution, in the Basic Law. And fundamentally this is the case. The federal state is governed by the federal constitution. However, the answers that the Basic Law gives are not always clear, sometimes incomplete, and moreover, they have been amended from time to time. Quite a few even think, like Dietrich Austermann (2019) quoted in the first chapter, that the

© Springer Fachmedien Wiesbaden GmbH, part of Springer Nature 2021
W. Reutter, *The German Länder*, https://doi.org/10.1007/978-3-658-33681-3_3

fathers and mothers of the Basic Law would have imagined a very different federal state than we have today. However, notwithstanding the amendments to the Basic Law, five constitutional principles are crucial for the design of the German federal state and the role that the *Länder* play in it. They shape the relationship between the federal government and the *Länder* and describe the framework for the political orders in the German subnational units (Vogel, 1995; Laufer & Münch, 2010, pp. 91–102; Leunig & Reutter, 2012; Münch, 2012; Reutter, 2021).

(1) Eternity clause: First to be mentioned is the eternity clause in Article 79 (3) BL. According to this clause, an amendment of the Basic Law "affecting the division of the Federation into *Länder*, their participation in principle in the legislative process, or the principles laid down in Articles 1 and 20 shall be inadmissible". The Federation and the *Länder* thus enjoy a comprehensive guarantee of existence. The federal state cannot be abolished as long as the Basic Law applies. This does not mean that *Länder* must remain within their existing borders (Sect. 2.2). Rather, the eternity clause only says that there must be a federal government and at least two *Länder*. Furthermore, the eternity clause stipulates that the *Länder* may participate in federal legislation. Currently, this is done through the *Bundesrat* (Federal Council), the representation of the *Länder* at the federal level (Sect. 7.1). However, federalism is also conceivable without such an eternity clause. But it points to the great importance that the constitutional fathers and mothers attached to this constitutional principle. Democracy and the federal state are constitutionally inseparable in the Federal Republic of Germany (Vogel, 1995, pp. 1049–1053; Laufer & Münch, 2010, pp. 26–29; Hesse, 1993, pp. 89–110). A concentration of political power in one instance and on one state level is thus excluded. According to the Basic Law, democracy can only be had as a federal state, and the federal state can only be democratic.

(2) Dual state structure: A second important principle is the dual structure of the federal state. What is meant by this is that both the federal government and the *Länder* possess state quality. What a state is, is not easy to define. The three-element doctrine of the constitutional lawyer Georg Jellinek (1851–1921) is widely used. According to Jellinek (1914, pp. 394–434), a state is characterized by three elements: by state people (*Staatsvolk*), by a state territory (*Staatsgebiet*), and by state power (*Staatsgewalt*) (Leunig & Reutter, 2012, pp. 746–752; Kriele, 1994, pp. 76–80). This concept of the state has been criticized for many reasons. It is not applicable to the *Länder*. Obviously the *Länder* do not enjoy unlimited state power. They cannot even independently determine who belongs to the people of the *Land*, because this is a federal matter. The federal government, through its legislation, directly affects the *Länder* and exercises state power there (just as the *Länder* participate in the exercise of state power at the federal level via the Bundesrat (Federal Council). However, the Federation and the *Länder* have the privilege of maintaining the institutions necessary for the exercise of state power, i.e. governments, administrations, parliaments and courts. And the *Länder* must have sufficient legislative powers and financial resources to perform their functions. The *Länder* are thus in principle on an equal footing with the Federation. At the same time, the Federation, as the supreme state, is superior to the *Länder*.

Competences according to state functions	Federal Government	*Länder*
Legislation	Almost all legislative powers (exclusive and concurrent legislation of the Federation)	Few legislative powers of its own (exclusive legislation of the *Länder*; police, education, municipal constitution etc.)
Administration	Few administrative powers of its own; mostly only legal supervision of the implementation of laws by the *Land* administrations	Almost all administrative powers; execution of almost all federal laws and *Land* laws
Jurisprudence	Seven federal courts (including the Federal Constitutional Court)	1,079 courts (including 16 *Land* constitutional courts)

Fig. 3.1 Division of competences between the Federal Government and the *Länder* according to the Basic Law. (*Source* Based on Bogumil & Jann, 2009, p. 76; own additions)

According to Article 31 of the Basic Law, federal law breaks *Land* law. Otherwise, a unity out of diversity, a republic of 16 equal and independent members cannot be established.

(3) The distribution of competences between the Federation and the Länder: Accompanying what has just been said is a third important constitutional principle: the division of powers between the Federation and the *Länder* (Fig. 3.1). The Basic Law seems unambiguous in this respect. It assumes a presumption of competence in favor of the *Länder* and postulates that the "exercise of state powers" and the "discharge of state functions is a matter for the *Länder*" (Art. 30 of the Basic Law). This fundamental all-embracing competence of the *Länder* is, however, subject to an important restriction. For it applies only "insofar as" the Basic Law does not provide otherwise. And this "insofar as", i.e. the exception, is in constitutional practice more important than the first-mentioned principle of universal competence. For the Basic Law has transferred a whole series of legislative competences to the Federation, while the *Länder* are mostly responsible for the execution of these laws—as "their own matter" (Art. 83 of the Basic Law) or on behalf of the Federation (Art. 85 of the Basic Law). In this context, it is also worth mentioning the provision that the Federation has the right to legislate in a number of areas "if and to the extent that the establishment of equivalent living conditions throughout the federal territory or the maintenance of legal or economic unity renders federal regulation necessary in the national interest" (Art. 72 (2) of the Basic Law).

The reform of federalism adopted in 2006 introduced some important changes in this area with the aim of separating competences between *Länder* and the Federation more clearly. For the *Länder* this meant above all that the legislative competence for some matters for which the Federation had previously been responsible was transferred to the *Länder* (civil service law, assembly law, penal system, salary law, nature conservation etc.). In addition, the possibility of "deviation legislation" was created for certain subjects of concurrent legislation and administrative matters (Art. 72 (3) and 84 of the Basic Law). According to this provision, the *Länder* may "enact laws at variance" with federal legislation in certain subjects (Art. 72 (3) of the Basic Law; see also Härtel, 2012; Schmidt-Jortzig, 2012; Laufer & Münch, 2010, pp. 115–136; Münch, 2019).

The division of competences between the Federation and the *Länder* thus follows primarily along state functions (not according to policy areas). Although there are also exceptions, this does not change the general principle of distribution: the Federation passes the (important) laws, the *Länder* execute these laws. This principle of distribution determines constitutional life and relations between the federal government and the *Länder*. This way of distributing competences along the functions of the state has far-reaching consequences, both in terms of democracy and control theory. We will return to this in a moment when we discuss theories on German federalism (Sect. 3.3). The *Länder* can legislate on their own authority in areas such as education, local government and policing, infrastructure and regional economic policy, foreigners and integration policy, the media, and transport and administrative policy. In addition, they adopt regulations to implement the laws passed by the *Bundestag* (Federal Diet).

(4) Homogeneity clause: The Basic Law not only regulates the relationship between the Federation and the *Länder* but also contains the so-called homogeneity clause. According to this clause, the constitutional order in the *Länder* must "conform to the principles of a republican, democratic and social state governed by the rule of law within the meaning of this Basic Law" (Art. 28 (1) of the Basic Law). "Conform" in this context does not mean "be identical". The constitutional orders of the *Länder* can therefore concretize the above-mentioned principles in different ways. Nevertheless, it is demanded without restriction that the *Länder* establish a republican system of government (a monarchy is just as impossible as an autocracy), that the exercise of state power is bound by the constitution and the law and can be controlled by independent courts (constitutional state) and that the citizens are granted a minimum of social security (social state). In each *Land*, moreover, parliament and government must come into being democratically. However, it remains open how the principle of democracy is implemented. In principle, the *Länder* are free to design their systems of government (Leunig, 2012, pp. 56–59). Here, then, unlike with the other principles mentioned, the *Länder* certainly have freedom of design. We will see whether they have used this freedom.

(5) Federal/Land friendly conduct: The fifth and final constitutional principle is not found directly in the Basic Law. It is unwritten constitutional law and results from rulings of the Federal Constitutional Court. According to it, the Federation and the *Länder* enter into a "reciprocal relationship of mutual trust", i.e. the Federation must act in a way that is friendly to the *Länder*, and the *Länder* must act in a friendly manner towards the other *Länder* and the Federation (Laufer & Münch, 2010, pp. 101 f.; Vogel, 1995, pp. 1061–1063). From this arises not only the duty to show consideration for each other, but the principle of federal comity implies that *Länder* cooperate, support each other (financially) in emergencies or

that administrations work together. Incidentally, the principle of federal-friendly conduct makes it impossible for a *Land* to leave the federal government. An exit of a *Land* from the Federal Republic of Germany is not possible.

3.2 *Land* Constitutions: The Political Orders in the *Länder*

Land constitutions regulate the internal order in the *Länder*. They may contain commitments to Europe or postulate that a *Land* is part of the Federal Republic of Germany. However, these are only constitutional provisions directed inwards. In addition, the Basic Law and federal laws have priority in principle (the only exception to this is the above-mentioned deviation legislation under Articles 72 and 84 of the Basic Law). This immediately raises the question of whether *Land* constitutions are not so "overshadowed by the Basic Law" (Möstl, 2005) that they have little or perhaps no effect on constitutional reality in the *Länder*. Even more: Are *Land* constitutions constitutions at all?[1]

A good constitution must be short and unclear. Short, so that it is easily manageable, and unclear, so that it can be interpreted as needed. This is a pithy and often quoted bon mot attributed to Napoléon Bonaparte (Simon, 2004, p. 406). Dieter Grimm (1994, p. 11) likes it more matter-of-fact. For him, a constitution regulates two things: the structure of the state and the relationship between society and the state. And Dieter Grimm should know. For he was a professor of public law and a judge at the Federal Constitutional Court from 1987 to 1999. All *Land* constitutions correspond to this definition—more or less. Moreover, a constitution should be adopted by the sovereign. After all, those to whom the constitution applies should have agreed to it. Constitution, in this perspective, is a social or governance contract entered into by the members of the political community. Such, at any rate, are the basic theoretical claims made for a legitimate constitution (Elster, 1994). In what follows, we want to examine whether and to what extent *Land* constitutions satisfy such claims and what their content is (Reutter, 2018b, 2021; Pestalozza, 2014a). First, let us look at the origins of *Land* constitutions (see Table 3.1).

In the present territory of the Federal Republic of Germany, a total of 24 *Land* constitutions have come into force since 1945.[2] This includes the five constitutions of the *Länder* in the Soviet occupation zone, which came into force in 1947, but which also became formally meaningless as early as 1952. In addition, the constitutions of Baden, Württemberg-Baden and Württemberg-Hohenzollern, which were adopted in 1946/1947, expired when the three *Länder* merged to form

---

[1]The following is based on Reutter (2008, pp. 45–68, 2018b, pp. 53–59).

[2]The Provisional Constitution of Greater Berlin adopted in 1948, the Provisional Constitution of the Hanseatic City of Hamburg of 1946, the *Land* constitution of Greater Hesse of 1945 and the provisional *Land* constitution of North Rhine-Westphalia of 1946 are not included; moreover, the Berlin Constitution, which entered into force in 1995, was not counted separately.

Table 3.1 Adoption of the *Land* constitutions in the western occupation zones and the east German *Länder*. (*Source* Reutter, 2008, p. 48)

Land	Entered into force on	Adoption of the Constitution by …			
		Constituent (in % of …)		Referendum (% of …)	
		Votes cast	Statutory members	Valid votes	Eligible voters
American occupation zone					
Bavaria	12/08/1946	90.7	75.5	70.6	49.6
Bremen	10/22/1947	96.4	81.0	72.4	45.1
Hesse	12/01/1946	93.2	91.1	76.8	48.8
Württemberg-Baden	[b](11/28/1946)	98.9	88.0	86.8	49.2
French occupation zone					
Baden	[b](05/22/1947)	76.9	65.5	67.9	42.8
Rhineland-Palatinate	05/18/1947	69.3	55.1	52.9	35.2
Saarland	12/17/1947	98.0	96.0	–	–
Württemberg-Hohenzollern	[b](05/20/1947)	80.7	70.8	69.8	43.6
British occupation zone					
Hamburg	07/01/1952	97.3	89.2	–	–
Lower Saxony	05/01/1951	77.5	71.8	–	–
North Rhine-Westphalia	07/11/1950	53.1	50.9	61.8	40.8
Schleswig–Holstein	01/12/1950	91.8	64.3	–	–
East German Länder[a]					
Brandenburg	08/21/1992	82.8	81.8	94.0	44.8
Mecklenburg-Western Pomerania	[c]05/23/1993	85.5	80.3	60.1	38.4
Saxony	06/06/1992	87.4	82.5	–	–
Saxony-Anhalt	07/18/1992	75.5	75.5	–	–
Thuringia	10/16/1994	84.6	84.1	74.2	50.5
Special cases					
Berlin	10/01/1950	100.0	80.0	[d]75.1	48.0
Baden-Württemberg	11/20/1953	89.5	64.2	–	–

[a]The Constitutions adopted in the *Länder* of the Soviet occupation zone in 1946/1947 became meaningless in June 1952

[b]The constitutions of Württemberg-Baden, Baden and Württemberg-Hohenzollern expired in 1953

[c]The Constitution of Mecklenburg-Western Pomerania entered into force provisionally on May 23, 1993, was confirmed by referendum on June 12, 1994 and entered into force definitively at the end of the first electoral period

[d]The referendum refers to the 1995 Constitution

Baden-Württemberg and a new *Land* constitution was adopted in 1953. The deliberation, adoption and approval of all *Land* constitutions followed—despite all the weighty differences in detail—a similar dramaturgy, which unfolded in three acts: pre-parliamentary phase—constituent assembly—decision (Pfetsch, 1990, pp. 29–61; Stiens, 1997, pp. 53–74; Reutter, 2008, p. 50; Hölscheidt, 1995).

Constitutional assemblies were only elected in the *Länder* of the American occupation zone. In the other *Länder*, the *Land* parliament (or a committee appointed by the *Land* parliament) took on the task of deliberation. In addition, in some *Land* parliaments the basic legal order was adopted by only a narrow majority (Table 3.1). In North Rhine-Westphalia, Schleswig–Holstein and Rhineland-Palatinate, fewer than two out of three elected members even voted in favor of the draft constitution submitted. Consequently, the constitutions were adopted by majorities smaller than would be required to amend them at a later date! In North Rhine-Westphalia, only just under 51% of the members of the *Land* parliament voted in favor of the draft submitted. Approval was even lower when a *Land* constitution was submitted to the voters for adoption. In the eight referendums that put *Land* constitutions into force, a clear majority of voters voted in favor of the respective draft. But in Thuringia alone, more than half of those eligible to vote voted in favor of the constitution, namely 50.5%. In the other *Länder*, the approval rate remained mostly well below the 50% mark. In Rhineland-Palatinate, the constitution was supported by just 35% of all eligible voters (Table 3.1). This certainly raises the question of whether such a referendum does not weaken rather than strengthen the "legitimacy and integrative power" of a constitution (Steinberg, 1992, p. 516) or whether a constitutional referendum is in any case only a kind of "democratic placebo" (Isensee, 1991, p. 219).

In addition to the question of how *Land* constitutions came into being, what is of particular interest is: What do *Land* constitutions say? And why do they differ? All *Land* constitutions contain provisions on state structure and political order (Table 3.2). All follow the basic outline of the Basic Law and establish a system in which the government is dependent on the *Land* parliament (Leunig, 2012). However, there are also important deviations, which will be discussed later (Chap. 6). Most *Land* constitutions also contain a catalogue of basic rights, some even basic duties, as well as provisions on state objectives and regulations on community life. They are therefore full constitutions. Only a few *Länder* have refrained from including fundamental rights in their constitutions. The constitution of Hamburg merely postulates that the Free and Hanseatic City is a "democratic and social constitutional *Land*" (Article 3 (1) of the Constitution of Hamburg). The differences between the *Land* constitutions can be traced back to two factors: the historical context in which they were created (a) and the party-political majorities in the constituent bodies (b).

(a) It is immediately noticeable that all *Land* constitutions that came into force before the Basic Law have a comprehensive catalogue of rights, duties and state objectives (Table 3.2). This is not surprising. For in 1946/47 it was still completely unclear what the Basic Law would look like. The *Land* constitutional assemblies therefore drew their lessons from Weimar—as did the Parliamentary Council

Table 3.2 *Land* constitutions: areas of regulation (original constitutions). (*Source* Lorenz & Reutter, 2013, p. 153; Flick, 2008, p. 224 f.)

Number of articles								Total (original constitution)
Basic rights Basic obligations, state objectives[a]		State organization[b]		State functions[c]		Other objects[d]		
# of articles	(%)	# of articles	(%)	# of articles	(%)	# of articles	%	# of articles
Land constitutions from the years 1946/47								
HES	65	(43.0)	41	(27.2)	35	(23.1)	10	(6.6)	151
BAV	93	(49.2)	47	(24.9)	38	(20.1)	11	(5.8)	189
BRE	69	(44.2)	53	(34.0)	28	(17.9)	6	(3.8)	156
SLD	65	(48.5)	33	(24.6)	31	(23.1)	5	(3.7)	134
RP	77	(53.1)	28	(19.3)	32	(22.1)	8	(5.5)	145
Land constitutions from the years 1950/1952								
SH	9	(15.0)	27	(45.0)	21	(35.0)	3	(5.0)	60
NRW	30	(32.3)	35	(37.8)	24	(25.8)	4	(4.3)	93
BER	38	(37.3)	21	(20.6)	37	(36.3)	6	(5.9)	102
LS	6	(7.7)	34	(43.6)	31	(39.7)	7	(9.0)	78
BW	27	(28.4)	31	(32.6)	27	(28.4)	10	(10.5)	95
HAM	6	(7.8)	42	(54.5)	25	(32.5)	4	(5.2)	77
Land constitutions from the years 1992/1993								
BB	55	(46.6)	34	(28.8)	25	(21.2)	4	(3.4)	118
MW	20	(24.7)	32	(39.5)	26	(32.1)	3	(3.7)	81
SAY	51	(41.5)	31	(25.2)	31	(25.2)	10	(8.1)	123
SAT	41	(40.2)	33	(32.4)	26	(25.5)	2	(2.0)	102
TH	48	(44.9)	31	(29.0)	25	(23.4)	3	(2.8)	107

[a]Basic rights and obligations, social life, objectives of the *Land*, foundations of the *Land*
[b]Regulations concerning the government and the *Land* parliament
[c]Legislative, executive (including finance), and judiciary
[d]Transitional and final provisions

later—and wanted to ensure that fundamental and human rights were guaranteed and that democracy was safeguarded. The initial situation was different in the *Länder* of the former British occupation zone. In these *Länder*, the constitutions were debated and adopted after the Basic Law had come into force. The constituent assemblies could therefore presuppose the fundamental and human rights contained in the Basic Law. They therefore concentrated on those parts concerning the *Land* organization or even merely adopted a "provisional constitution" (Lower Saxony) or a so-called "statute" (Schleswig–Holstein), both of which were almost devoid of independent fundamental rights. The constitutions of Baden-Württemberg and North Rhine-Westphalia also contain only a few provisions on fundamental rights (Art. 1–3 of the Constitution of Baden-Württemberg and Art. 4 of the Constitution of North Rhine-Westphalia), but comparatively many on the social and economic order, which in turn is largely unregulated in the Basic Law.

The case of Berlin was somewhat different. Admittedly, according to the Basic Law and the Berlin Constitution of 1 September 1950, Berlin was "a *Land* of the Federal Republic of Germany" (Art. 1 (2) of the Berlin Constitution). However, the *Land* was under Allied reservation. It was not allowed to be governed directly from the federal government. Federal laws therefore contained a so-called "Berlin clause", which stipulated that the respective law should also apply in Berlin. In addition, the Berlin House of Representatives had to pass a separate resolution to adopt each federal law. The Constitution of Berlin (VvB), adopted by the House of Representatives in 1950, therefore contained a comprehensive catalogue of fundamental rights and was intended to extend at the same time to the eastern part of the city, i.e. the capital of the GDR.

The constitutions of the eastern German *Länder* that came into force between 1992 and 1994, are also full constitutions, in some cases with extensive catalogues of fundamental rights and provisions on state objectives. Only the constitution of Mecklenburg-Western Pomerania contains few fundamental rights and makes with Article 5 (3) of the Constitution of Mecklenburg West-Pomerania—like the constitutions of Baden-Württemberg, Lower Saxony and North Rhine-Westphalia—the basic rights and civic obligations set out in the Basic Law of the Federal Republic of Germany an "integral part" of the *Land* constitution.

The provisions on direct democracy were also directly influenced by the context in which they were created. While the *Land* constitutions, which are older than the Basic Law, granted the "people" the possibility of authoritatively deciding on laws from the very beginning, the other *Länder* created this possibility only gradually (Sect. 4.2).

(b) In addition to the historical context, the party-political majorities in the constitution-making bodies were especially important for the content of the *Land* constitutions (Reutter, 2008, pp. 49–53, 2018b, pp. 53–59; Pfetsch, 1990): on the one hand, the parties held different ideological views, which were reflected in the *Land* constitutions (Pfetsch, 1985, p. 133). While, for example, in the Christian Democrat-dominated southern German *Länder*, fundamental Christian values were given a prominent role in the *Land* constitutions, in social democratic-governed *Länder* such as Hesse and Bremen, it was primarily the economic and social order that was given constitutional shape. However, such ideological basic positions could by no means be transferred into constitutional law without further ado. On the other hand, at the time of the drafting of the constitution, no party in any *Land* had a two-thirds majority, which, however, was not always necessary for the adoption of the draft constitution in parliament. However, in many cases the desire to obtain the greatest possible approval for the constitution led to compromises between the parties.

3.3   *Länder* and Federalism: Theoretical Approaches

According to André Kaiser (2012, p. 166), theories of federalism should provide answers to three questions: Why are federal systems established? How do they maintain their stability and adaptability? And how efficient are they? According to Henrik Scheller (2016), there is so far no political science theory of federalism that provides answers to all three questions. This may be partly because the causes, functional conditions, and performance of federal states are difficult to capture in a single theoretical concept. With a somewhat more modest claim, it can therefore be said that political science theories of federalism should attempt to explain the preconditions, functioning, and consequences of the democratic federal state. They should therefore examine at least four dimensions: first, the connection between democratic order and federal structure; second, the processes of political will-formation and decision-making in German-style cooperative federalism; third, the questions of whether and to what extent the federal state promotes or impairs the capacity for action and control; and finally, fourth, the significance of the *Länder* in each of these dimensions (see also Behnke, 2015).

This, too, is an ambitious undertaking that is not made any easier against the background of the constitutional foundations outlined. It should therefore come as no surprise that the aforementioned questions have been considered from different perspectives. Dietmar Braun (2004, p. 131), in an overview article, lists five "most important theoretical approaches" in—comparative—federalism research alone. Braun then subdivides these "most important" approaches once again into 16 subvariants, and Braun does not even claim to be exhaustive (Braun, 2004, p. 131).

Helms et al. (2017, pp. 544–549) also distinguish five major theoretical debates that could be found in the "German school" of—again comparative—federalism research. I follow this classification in the remainder of this chapter but limit myself to those approaches that deal solely or predominantly with federalism in the Federal Republic of Germany. I thus neglect concepts that examine the European multi-level system from a federalism-theoretical perspective or that look at the federal state from a financial-scientific point of view. On this basis, three "schools" can be distinguished, which cannot always be clearly separated from each other.

(1) Democracy and federalism: The first political science reflections on the federal state focused on the relationship between democracy and federalism. In this perspective—following the American constitutional debate of 1777/1778—federalism is interpreted as a structure that divides powers and is primarily intended to safeguard democracy. Federalism is supposed to prevent an abuse of state power, to make the establishment of an authoritarian regime impossible (or at least more difficult), and to enable citizens to participate politically at different levels (Sturm, 2015; Steffani, 1990, 1999). Democracy and federalism necessarily belong together in this perspective. Federal states are democratic states, according to the credo of this school, which, however, is no longer entirely uncontroversial (Benz & Kropp, 2014) and is also quite critically discussed for the German case, as the two dominant approaches show (Benz, A. 2009).

(2) Intertwined policy-making (Politikverflechtung) and the *structural break hypothesis (Strukturbruchthese)*: The constitutional lawyer Konrad Hesse, as mentioned above, steered the debate in a new direction in the early 1960s. In his 1962 treatise on the "unitary federal state", he drew attention to the fact that German federalism was characterized by internal contradictions: For the fundamentally decentralized and power-sharing structure of the federal state was being undermined by tendencies toward unitarization and centralization. There was the constitutional duty to create "uniform" or—since 1994—"equivalent" living conditions (Art. 72 (2) of the Basic Law), and in addition the Federation had legislative competence in all important areas. In conjunction with the idea, widespread in the 1970s, that the state could shape society and the economy in a goal-oriented manner, this constitutional reinterpretation has had a lasting impact on the political science debate on the structure and functioning of the federal state. The two most important approaches can be described and personalized with the above-mentioned terms "intertwined policymaking" and "structural break": The concept of "intertwined policymaking" is linked to Fritz W. Scharpf, while the "structural break" hypothesis was developed by Gerhard Lehmbruch.

Gerhard Lehmbruch's study on "Party Competition in the Federal State", first published in 1976, has received much attention (Helms, 2007a). He published this study again in a third, heavily revised edition in 2000. He examines—as the title of the book announces—the relationship between party competition and the federal state and concludes that both function according to different "logics" or rules: The party system is based on competition and operates with majority decisions, the federal state requires cooperation and leads to compromises (Lehmburch, 2000, p. 19). According to Lehmbruch, these two logics are incongruent and lead either to a "legitimacy gap" (so 1976) or to an "effectiveness gap" (so Lehmbruch, 2000; see Helms, 2007a). Legitimacy problems can arise because democratic party competition is restricted or undermined, because federal states, via the Bundesrat (Federal Council), prevent the elected federal government from implementing its program legitimised in elections, and because results of political decisions can no longer be clearly attributed. Effectiveness problems can arise because compromise constraints lead to decisions that are inadequate to the problem and can prevent necessary reforms. In any case, the assumption discussed above that federalism and democracy complement and stabilize each other seems at least questionable (Kropp, 2010, pp. 56–61).

It is certainly no coincidence that Fritz W. Scharpf, Bernd Reissert and Fritz Schnabel (1976) presented their study on intertwined policymaking in the same year as Gerhard Lehmbruch presented his study on party competition in the federal state. Curiously enough, Scharpf, Reissert and Schnabel did not primarily want to explain policy gridlocks in German federalism with their study. Rather, they addressed questions of control theory and wanted to know how the state can govern effectively in a certain area—in so-called common tasks. But the conclusions from this study were quickly generalized and developed into a general theory of intertwined policymaking (Kropp, 2010). This approach can be used to identify causes of problems in systems in which decision-making powers are distributed across different levels. Such a constellation produces—in generalized form—a trap of "intertwined policymaking" (Scharpf, 1985). It refers to a decision-making structure linking two or more levels which, due to its institutional logic, "produces inefficient and inappropriate decisions" and is at the same time incapable of "changing the institutional conditions of its decision-making process" (Scharpf, 1985, p. 350).

This was and is a highly influential approach that could be used to explain all sorts of problems. Reform gridlock, policy blockades, and "policies of the middle way" (Schmidt, 1990, 1987) have become popular buzzwords in this context, prompting one German president (Roman Herzog, 1997) to call for a "jolt" to go through the country and another (Horst Köhler, 2005, p. 1) to make the apodictic judgment: "The existing federal order is outdated." The federalism reform passed in 2006 was supposed to solve this problem and to disentangle responsibilities between the federal and *Land* governments, increase the transparency of political decision-making processes, and improve the state's ability to act. Or in the words of Matthias Platzeck, one of the many former leaders of the SPD: ruling was to become "faster, more efficient and better" (quoted from Burkhart & Manow, 2006, p. 2; see also Reutter, 2006b; Scharpf, 2009; Kropp, 2010, pp. 209–237; Münch, 2019; Behnke & Kropp, 2016).

(3) Länder and federalism: It is noticeable that in the approaches presented so far the *Länder* appear primarily in their federal role. This is plausible. For in the "unitary federal state" the *Länder* play a role primarily in their constitutional quality. And in this respect, they are all equal, apart from the fact that *Länder* have different numbers of votes in the *Bundesrat* (Federal Council). The differences between *Länder* only became more prominent after German unification and were then reflected in corresponding theoretical debates (Hildebrandt & Wolf, 2016a, 2006a). However, a unified theory to explain politics in the *Länder* has not yet been established. Three approaches dominate: First, political systems in the *Länder* are analyzed using approaches developed in comparative systems research that revolve around the question of whether and to what extent the systems of government in *Länder* correspond to those in the federal government (Leunig, 2012; Freitag & Vatter, 2008). Second, with the so-called "party difference hypothesis", the role of parties is addressed. Here, the aim is to work out whether and to what extent policy outcomes can be traced back to the composition of *Land* governments and *Land* parliaments (Schmidt, 1980). Finally, different policy fields are examined on the basis of policy analyses. The aim here is to work out how policy outcomes come about (Hildebrandt & Wolf, 2006b, 2016b). In addition, there are studies on individual institutions such as parliaments (Reutter, 2008, 2017a), direct democratic procedures (Jung, 2012; Kost, 2005), *Land* parties (Jun et al., 2008; Kost et al., 2010), and *Land* constitutional courts (Reutter, 2017b, 2020a, b) as well as fiscal studies (Renzsch, 2000; Anderson & Scheller, 2012; Hildebrandt, 2016), which deal in particular with the system of fiscal equalization.

Representative and Direct Democracy in the *Länder*: Complement or Contradiction?

4

Abstract

The chapter presents the electoral systems and direct democratic procedures in the *Länder*. The guiding questions of this chapter are: How do elections direct democracy work in the *Länder*? What functions do they fulfil? And how do the two central forms of democratic participation relate to each other?

4.1 Elections and Democracy in the *Länder*

When the term democracy is to be defined, Abraham Lincoln, the 16th president of the USA, is often quoted. Lincoln took office in 1861, was re-elected in 1864, and fell victim to an assassination attempt in 1865. He held office during the American Civil War (1861–1865). His achievement, which cannot be overestimated to this day, was to have constitutionally banned slavery with the inclusion of the 13th Amendment in 1865, to have prevented the secession of the Southern States (the Confederate States of America), and thus to have preserved the unity of the United States of America. Abraham Lincoln, in this context and after the Battle of Gettysburg in 1863, delivered a speech that was as short as it was famous. At the conclusion of his *Gettysburg Address, which* was just 272 words long, Lincoln invoked the unity of the American nation. The nation, he said, shall have "under God [...] a new birth of freedom—and that government of the people, by the people, for the people, shall not perish from the earth". And this "government of the people, by the people, for the people" was to become a democratic bedrock as firm as it is timeless. What it is supposed to mean, Lincoln did not explain. Consequently, it allows for different interpretations. But the "people," whoever may be included, have an almost religious status in this formulation. In any case, this implies that all public officials entrusted with the administration of state affairs must have democratic legitimacy (Böckenförde, 1992, p. 302).

© Springer Fachmedien Wiesbaden GmbH, part of Springer Nature 2021
W. Reutter, *The German Länder*, https://doi.org/10.1007/978-3-658-33681-3_4

This requirement has found expression in the *Land* constitutions. In them, state power also emanates from the figure of the "people". However, state power is exercised in "elections and ballots and through special organs of legislation, executive power and jurisdiction" (Art. 25 (1) of the Constitution of Baden-Württemberg). This not only stipulates the principle of separation of powers (Chap. 6). Rather, it also means that in the *Länder* the sovereign must be able to periodically elect members to the *Land* parliament. In addition, it can act as legislator. Unlike in the federal government, both forms of political participation are consequently possible and provided for in the *Länder*. The participation of the sovereign in the formation of the will of the state in the *Länder* is complicated by the fact that this takes place in a federal state. Thus, the peoples of the *Länder* are not sovereign in the strict sense of that word. This is to be taken into account in the further presentation. It should also be mentioned in advance that there are other forms of political participation (demonstrations, etc.), which will not be discussed.

The homogeneity clause in Article 28 (1) of the Basic Law, which has already been cited several times, stipulates that in the *Länder* "the people shall be represented by a body chosen in general, direct, free, equal and secret elections". This provision is an outgrowth of the principle of democracy, which is endowed with a guarantee of perpetuity and is found in all *Land* constitutions. Democracy is understood here as representative democracy in which representatives are elected to make decisions that are binding on all (Fraenkel, 1991, pp. 152–203; Schüttemeyer 1995). For such a broad mandate to be justified, elections to *Land* parliaments must be fair and free. This applies to all elections of representatives to democratic representative bodies. For in the *Länder*, members are not only elected for *Land* parliaments, but also for the European Parliament, the *Bundestag* (Federal Diet) or for municipal bodies. And different rules apply to the respective elections. Brandenburg is a case in point (Table 4.1). In this *Land*, for example, voting in *Land* and local elections is possible at the age of 16 (in federal and European elections at the age of 18); in EU and local elections, citizens of EU member states can vote (otherwise only German citizens); in *Land* and federal elections there is a five-percent hurdle (which does not exist in European and local elections); in European elections voters can cast one vote (in *Land* and federal elections two votes and in local elections even three votes). Voters in Brandenburg were able to take part in a total of 28 elections between October 3, 1990, the day on which Brandenburg became part of the Federal Republic of Germany, and the end of 2019. The rest of the presentation is limited to the elections to *Land* parliaments.

In democracies, elections are the most important legitimation procedure. They are supposed to provide the constitutional bodies and the mandate holders or office holders with the justification to exercise state power in the name of and on behalf of the "people". However, as we know from history and hear almost daily in the news, this connection between free and fair elections and a stable democratic order is by no means compelling. It depends on a whole series of preconditions. For example, a sufficient number of voters should take part in elections; at the same time, the election results should allow a government to be formed. For democracy

Table 4.1 Electoral law and electoral systems in Brandenburg (as of December 2019). (*Source* Reutter, 2016b, p. 60; own addition; https://www.wahlrecht.de. Accessed: December 5, 2019. http://www.wahlen.brandenburg.de/. Accessed: December 5, 2019)

	European elections	Federal elections	*Land* elections	Local elections
Regulatory level	European/ National	National	*Land*	*Land*
Voting age (active/passive)	18/18	18/18	16/18	16/18
Nationality	EU	German	German	EU
Election system	Proportional representation	Personalized proportional representation	Personalized proportional representation	Proportional representation
Vote Count	1	2	2	3
5-percent hurdle	No	Yes[a]	Yes	No
Basic mandate clause	No	3 direct mandates[a]	1 direct mandate	No
Compensatory mandates	No	Yes	Yes	No
Seat allocation procedure	Sainte-Laguë	Sainte-Laguë	Hare/Niemeyer	Hare/Niemeyer
Number of elections since 10/1990	6	8	7	6

[a]In relation to the whole of Germany

means not only that the sovereign can participate, but also that it can be governed effectively. Elections would be meaningless if they were exhausted in the act of participation. In the *Länder*, both requirements have been taken into account.

The principles of electoral law guarantee that fair and free, and thus democratic, elections can take place. All elections in the *Länder* are also subject to the principles of electoral law set out in the Basic Law (Article 38). They are thus to be universal, free, equal, direct and secret. This is to ensure that as large a proportion of the population as possible participates in elections, that open competition for electoral votes is possible, that every vote counts equally, and that voting can take place anonymously and covertly (Marschall, 2005, pp. 42–46; Nohlen, 2000, pp. 37–39; Reutter, 2008, pp. 73–75). These voting principles, which are reiterated in the *Land* constitutions, can change. For example, in the 1950s and 1960s, voting in the *Länder* was only possible from the age of 21, then at 18, and now the age for voting has been lowered to 16 in some *Länder*. The lowering of the voting age was intended to make elections more "universal".

Electoral laws define who can vote and how, and who may be elected and how (Nohlen, 2000, pp. 37–39; Korte, 2003, p. 10.12; Marschall, 2005, pp. 42–46).

Table 4.2 Electoral systems in the *Länder* (as of 2019). (*Source* https://www.wahlrecht.de/land-tage/index.html. Accessed: April 23, 2019)

Land	Term length (years)	Mandates (direct)	Compensatory mandates[a]	Vote counts[a]	Five percent hurdle	Basic mandate clause[a]
BW	5	120 (70)	Yes	1	Yes	No
BAY	5	180 (91)	Yes	2	Yes	No
BER	5	130 (78)	Yes	2	Yes	one mandate
BB	5	88 (44)	Yes	2	Yes[b]	one mandate
BRE	4	84 (0)	No	5	Yes[c]	No
HAM	5	121 (71)	Yes	10	Yes	No
HES	5	110 (55)	Yes	2	Yes	No
MW	5	71 (36)	Yes	2	Yes	No
LS	5	135 (87)	Yes	2	Yes	No
NRW	5	181 (128)	Yes	2	Yes	No
RP	5	101 (51)	Yes	2	Yes	No
SLD	5	51 (0)	No	1	Yes	No
SAY	5	120 (60)	Yes	2	Yes	two mandates
SAT	5	83 (41)	Yes	2	Yes	No
SH	5	69 (35)	Yes	2	Yes[d]	one mandate
TH	5	88 (44)	Yes	2	Yes	No

[a]See explanations in the text
[b]In Brandenburg, the five per cent threshold does not apply to the Sorbian minority
[c]In Bremen the five percent hurdle applies separately in the two electoral constituencies Bremen and Bremerhaven
[d]in Schleswig–Holstein the Danish minority is exempt from the five per cent threshold (SSW)

Thus, the conditions for the right to vote and to stand for election are formulated. The question of how the votes cast become a parliamentary assembly is different. For the result of the vote can be converted differently into parliamentary mandates. In a purely majoritarian electoral system, as exists in Britain, the candidate who has received the most votes in her constituency wins the mandate. This is called a "first-past-the-post" electoral system. The same mechanism applies in *Länder* for MPs who are directly elected in constituencies. In the *Länder* these are currently 895 out of a total of at least 1740 MPs (excluding overhang and compensatory mandates). This means that more than half of all MPs to be elected are elected according to this principle (Table 4.2).

Nevertheless: In the German *Länder*, it is not the majoritarian system but the proportional representation system that applies. In most *Länder*, proportional representation is merely "personalized", because candidates are elected directly in constituencies. But personalization does not change the fact that the strength of the parties should be reflected in the composition of parliaments. A proportional representation system is thus intended to ensure that political parties are represented in parliament as proportionally as possible (Nohlen, 2000, pp. 121–161). All *Land* electoral systems follow this principle of "proportional representation" (Nohlen, 2000, p. 136 f.). However, the *Länder* apply this principle in different ways (Table 4.2):

- In Bremen and Saarland there are no constituency candidates. Here, the voters can only cast their votes for parties that run with lists on which their candidates are listed. In these *Länder*, therefore, not personalized but pure proportional representation applies.
- In a proportional representation system, the five-percent hurdle is a foreign element. This hurdle, found in all *Länder*, means that a party is only represented in parliament if it receives at least five percent of the second votes. If it receives less than five percent, it is not represented in parliament. These votes are then lost. They do not count for the calculation of the distribution of seats in parliament—unless a party represents a minority (in BB and SH) or one or two of its candidates have won a seat in a constituency. This is the so-called basic mandate clause (*Grundmandatsklausel*). Then the party enters parliament in the strength with which it has performed in the election. An example: The party BVB/Freie Wähler received 2.7% of the second votes in the 2014 *Land* election in Brandenburg, so on the basis of this result it would not have been represented in the *Land* parliament because of the five-percent hurdle. However, because its leading candidate Christoph Schulze had won the direct mandate in the constituency of Teltow-Fläming, the party was allocated three seats in parliament because of the basic mandate clause (the directly won mandate plus two list mandates; Niedermayer, 2015, p. 29 f.).
- With the exception of Bremen and Saarland, overhang and compensatory mandates can occur in *Land* elections. Overhang mandates (*Überhangmandate*) arise when a party has won more constituencies in an election to a *Land* parliament than it would have been entitled to according to the results of the second vote. Such overhang mandates are compensated for in the 14 *Länder* in which they can occur, until the strength ratio in parliament corresponds to the vote shares.
- In Baden-Württemberg and Saarland, voters have only one vote, although in Baden-Württemberg they vote for both a constituency candidate and a party. In Saarland, they can only vote for one party anyway. In Bremen and Hamburg, voters have five and ten votes respectively, which they can distribute as they wish among candidates in constituencies (Hamburg) or on party lists (Bremen and Hamburg).

These differences do not change the fact that in all *Länder* the proportional representation system applies, which in principle favors the emergence of a multi-party system. We will see in the next chapter whether and to what extent evidence for this "law" formulated by Maurice Duverger (1959, p. 219; Nohlen, 2000, pp. 395–397) in the 1950s can be found in the *Länder*. At this point, it is rather of interest whether and to what extent elections and electoral systems in the *Länder* were able to fulfil their functions. Three basic functions can be distinguished for this purpose: (a) legitimacy of the political order, (b) representativeness of election results, and (c) to what extent elections lead to stable governments, i.e. the electoral system has concentration effects (Korte, 2003, p. 10; Reutter, 2008, pp. 89–97; Nohlen, 2000, pp. 157–159).

(a) Legitimacy (voter turnout): What is meant by this is that the "totality of citizens" should be represented (Korte, 2003, p. 10). On election nights, media not only report on successes and failures of parties, but they also make reference to how high the turnout was. And then the Olympic motto seems to apply: higher, faster, stronger. If the turnout is lower than in the last election, this is taken as evidence of disenchantment with politics or even democracy. If it is higher, it means that the voters were satisfied with politics and the political order. However, "voter turnout" as an indicator is "less meaningful than one might initially think" (Nohlen, 2000, p. 159). For high voter turnout can also be an expression of dissatisfaction or even an outflow of a fundamentally critical attitude towards democracy. In 2018/2019, for example, voter turnout increased in all elections to *Land* parliaments, but this was mainly due to the AfD, which was able to mobilize many non-voters. The success of right-wing populist or in some respects even right-wing extremist parties can hardly be interpreted as a stabilizing factor for democracy. At the same time, abstinence from voting can be a reaction to the fact that voters are satisfied. What does not exist, by the way, is the party of non-voters. Non-voters are just as heterogeneous as voters. What they want, we do not know.

However, irrespective of these considerations, three observations can be made with regard to voter turnout in the *Länder*: on average, it was lower in *Land* elections than in federal elections; for the period from 1946 to 2007, the difference was almost 10% points. It has been cyclical, peaking at an average of just under 80% in the 1960s and 1970s, falling to around 66% thereafter, and averaging around 65% in recent elections to *Land* parliaments (as of 2019). It is usually lower in the east German *Länder* than in the west German ones (Reutter, 2008, p. 91). But, as I said, as clear and unambiguous as the empirical findings may be, it is unclear how these findings are to be classified and evaluated. In any case, it is true that no democracy has ever perished from too low a voter turnout.

This corresponds to another development: the legitimacy of elections depends not only on voter turnout, but also on how many residents are eligible to vote.[1] In the 2017 *Land* elections in North Rhine-Westphalia, this was just 47.9%. Of this, the governing parties CDU and FDP received 45.6%. In other words, the coalition that has been in power in NRW since 2017 represents around 46% of voters, 30% of eligible voters and 22% of the population!

---

[1]Residents are all persons who are registered in a *Land,* a municipality or another territorial authority. Nationality, which is important for eligibility to vote, plays no role here, nor does age.

(b) Representativeness: Elections are the easiest way to actively participate in politics. Ignoring the question of what citizens base their voting decision on, the effort for this democratic act is limited. One either casts one's vote on election day or does so by mailing the ballot. However, elections lose their democratic quality if certain groups are systematically under- or over-represented. Everyone must have the same opportunity and be able to exert the same influence on politics. "One man (person), one vote!" This historic rallying cry memorably illustrates the demand for political equality. In all *Länder*, this equality postulate is constitutionally guaranteed. In principle, every vote counts the same; there is no three-class voting system or the like. All votes are supposed to have the same "counting value", as the Federal Constitutional Court has emphasized repeatedly.

Equal voting rights, however, do not yet mean equal influence in elections. This is because participation varies systematically and permanently between social groups. "Democracy becomes a matter for the better-off", as Wolfgang Merkel (2019) pointedly put it in an interview. In several studies, the Bertelsmann Stiftung always comes to the same findings and to a similar conclusion as Merkel: although participation in the elections in Bremen and Hamburg (2015) and in NRW (2017) has increased in each case compared to the last election, the social divide has rather worsened. Thus, voter turnout in the economically stronger milieus is significantly higher than in economically weaker constituencies. The authors of these studies therefore speak of "precarious elections" and of "divided democracy" and state that, under the above-mentioned conditions, the people's representations can no longer claim to be socially representative (Bertelsmann Stiftung, 2015a, b, 2017).

(c) Concentration (ability to govern): Elections should lead to governments. For political self-determination—and democracy is nothing else—is not exhausted by participation but includes the ability to shape a society in a goal-oriented way. For this, a government must be elected and supported on a permanent basis. An electoral system can help to accomplish this task. The first-past-the-post electoral system, for example, is considered particularly effective in this respect because it favors two-party systems and thus facilitates the formation of governments. For example, the Tories (with Boris Johnson as their leading candidate) received just 43.6% of the votes cast in the 2019 elections to the House of Commons, but 55.7% of the seats in the House of Commons because of the electoral system. Until the recent past, however, it was also quite possible to form a government in the German *Länder* (see also Sect. 6.1). Between 1946 and 2007, in 87 of 199 *Land* elections, one party alone achieved a parliamentary majority, i.e. was able to govern without a coalition partner (Reutter, 2008, p. 96). In 32 of these cases this majority was due to the electoral system. In these cases, less than 50% of the second votes were sufficient for a parliamentary majority. In NRW, too, the CDU and FDP together received only about 46% of the second votes in the 2017 *Land* election. However, since some parties failed to clear the five-percent hurdle and the votes cast for these parties were not used to calculate parliamentary mandates, the CDU and FDP had a one-vote majority in the *Land* parliament. However, this example should not obscure the fact that the arrival of the AfD in all *Land* parliaments has made the formation of governments much more difficult and can lead to unstable coalitions.

4.2   Direct Democracy in the *Länder*

In the *Länder*, governance "of the people, by the people, for the people" includes not only the election of representatives, but also that voters can vote on bills themselves. Thus, representative and direct forms of democratic participation coexist.

"Direct democracy" is an iridescent term and a fuzzy concept (Jung, 2012; Heußner & Jung, 1999; Rehmet, 2019). What exactly is covered by it is interpreted differently (Fig. 4.1). Some argue that only initiatives that originate "from below" should be considered direct democratic procedures. Others are somewhat more generous and also include consultations, referenda or referendums initiated "from above", i.e. by parliaments or governments. The binding nature of the decision also plays a role. For example, Popular consultation and petitions or initiatives by the people have no binding effect on the government or parliaments. Popular initiatives "force" parliaments to deal with the subject of the initiative, but beyond that they have no legal consequences (unless the initiative is also the first stage of popular legislation).

The crown of direct democracy is considered to be the popular legislation, because the sovereign can decide in its own matter (Rehmet, 2019, p. 6 f.). In the *Länder*, this includes a "petition for a referendum", which can also be submitted as a popular initiative, the referendum itself, and the final referendum. Between the petition and the decision, the parliament has the opportunity to consider the bill, adopt it if necessary, or submit an alternative bill for a vote. It is certainly not surprising that *Länder* have designed these stages differently. The number of signatures required at each stage varies, as does the method of collection or the time period in which signatures must be collected (Table 4.3). In this regard, Christina Eder and Raphael Magin (2008, p. 307) conclude in their study of direct democratic procedures in the *Länder* that "the different procedural requirements

		Initiators	
		From above (government, parliament)	From below (voters)
Binding	Non-binding	Popular consultation, popular petitions	People's initiative
	Binding	Plebiscite, referendum	Popular legislation (petition for referendum and popular referendum)

Fig. 4.1 Types of direct-democratic procedures according to binding nature and initiators. (*Source* my compilation)

Table 4.3 Referendums and plebiscites in the *Länder*: introduction, procedural rules and number (as of 2018). (*Source* own compilation; Rehmet, 2019, p. 12 and p. 16 f.)

	Introduction	People's petition			Referendums		
		Quorum (%)[a]	Registration deadline (Office/ Free)[b]	Count	Simple law (in %)	Constitutional amendment (%)	Number
BW	1974	10	6 months (O/F)	0 (9)	20	50	0
BAV	1946	10	14 days (O)	20 (57)	No quorum	25	6
BER	1995	7 (20)	4 months (O/F)	10 (35)	25	50 + 2/3 majority	9
BB	1992	Approx. 3.8	6 months (O)	14 (49)	25	50 + 2/3 majority	0
BRE	1947	5 (10)	3 months (F)	4 (14)	20	40	0
HAM	1996	5	21 days (O)	16 (50)	20	(-) + 2/3 majority	7
HES	1946	5	2 months (O)	1 (7)	25	Not possible	0
MW	1994	7,5[c]	5 months (F)	4 (29)	25	50 + 2/3 majority	1
LS	1993	10	6 months (F)	3 (10)	25	50	0
NRW	1950	8	12 months (O/F)	3 (14)	15	50 + 2/3 majority	0
RP	1947	9,7[d]	2 months (O)	1 (6)	25	50	0
SLD	1979	7	3 months (O)	2 (8)	25	50 + 2/3 majority	0
SAY	1992	13,2[e]	8 months (F)	4 (14)	No quorum	50	1
SAT	1992	9	6 months (F)	3 (3)	25[c]	50 + 2/3 majority	1
SH	1990	3,6	6 months (O)	5 (36)	15	50 + 2/3 majority	2
TH[c]	1994	10	4 months (F)	5 (10)	25	40	0

[a]Signature quorum; in brackets the signature quorum for laws amending the constitution; in BB, MW, RP, SAY and SH the required number of signatures was converted into shares of voters, the reference values may vary: in Berlin and Brandenburg the quorums refer to residents of full age, otherwise to those entitled to vote or to stand in elections

[b]A distinction is made as to whether the signatures are to be registered in a public office or can be collected freely; in some cases both variants are possible; in BB and HAM registration by letter is also possible

[c]The quorum for approval does not apply if the turnout is 50% or more

[d]In Thuringia there were an additional 8 citizens' applications

[e]In brackets: Number of popular initiatives

are a major factor in explaining the frequency of use of direct participation instruments." In somewhat simpler terms, this means that the lower the hurdles, the more referendum petitions and referendums there have been.

As mentioned, all *Land* constitutions now provide for the possibility of direct democratic participation and popular legislation (see further Reutter, 2013, pp. 90–99; Rehmet, 2019; Jung, 2012). Notwithstanding the differences in detail, the following conclusions can be drawn (Table 4.3):

- First, the possibility of popular legislation was successively expanded. When the Basic Law came into force, four *Land* constitutions included direct-democratic procedures, and three more had been added by the time of unification in 1990. Berlin had provided for direct democratic procedures in its 1950 constitution, but never passed the necessary implementing law. Only the electorates in Hamburg and Lower Saxony were denied the possibility of initiating referendums and deciding independently on draft laws until 1990. Together with the east German *Länder* and Berlin, however, these two *Länder* also amended their constitutions in the 1990s and enabled procedures initiated "from below". Added to these extensions were procedural simplifications (fewer signatures, more time to collect).
- Secondly, almost all *Land* constitutions contain taboos: the financial taboo, i.e. the prohibition of referendums concerning the state budget, taxes or levies, is well known. Inadmissible are usually also procedures concerning service and pension payments as well as the state personnel.
- Thirdly, as a rule of thumb, the more binding the decision, the higher the hurdle. Thus, the quorums (i.e. the number of signatures required) for popular initiatives range between 0.1 and 2%, for petitions for referendums between 3.8 and 13.2%, and for referendums usually at least 15 or 25% of those eligible to vote must approve the draft (plus the majority of those voting). Only in Bavaria and Saxony is there no approval quorum, while in Rhineland-Palatinate at least 25% of those eligible to vote must take part in the referendum. In the case of laws amending the constitution, the approval quorums are even higher. In addition, a draft bill must be submitted, which can be examined by the state government or the constitutional court for its constitutionality.
- Fourthly, direct democratic procedures have become less attractive with unification. According to the non-governmental association "Mehr Demokratie e.V.", which keeps meticulous records of all direct democratic procedures and initiatives, of the 420 procedures initiated from below between 1946 and the end of 2018, only 28 were initiated before 1990; the rest (392) were started between 1990 and 2018 (Rehmet, 2019, p. 15).
- Fifthly, if one follows the surveys of "Mehr Demokratie e.V.", just 13 out of a total of 330 procedures turned out in the initiators' favour (=3.9%). If an extended definition of success is used, the figure is 28.5% (Rehmet, 2019, p. 24). Thus, 236 procedures failed because not enough signatures could be collected, the petition was withdrawn, declared inadmissible or the required majority was not reached.

- Sixth, participation in referendums is significantly lower than in elections. On average, only a little more than one-third of eligible voters go to the polls for referendums. Excluding votes held at the same time as *Land* elections, an average of 34.1% of eligible voters participated in referendums for bottom-up initiatives and 34.9% for mandatory referendums (Rehmet, 2019, p. 37). In addition, low participation greatly favors certain groups and disadvantages others. Moreover, it excludes all those who do not have the right to vote.

It can hardly be emphasized often enough: In the *Länder*, voters can not only elect their representatives to parliaments, but they can also make substantive decisions and in some cases even dissolve parliament (which has never been carried out to the point of voting). This is a qualitative difference between the federal government and the *Länder*. And this difference is not trivial. In Bavarian politics, the possibility of holding referendums and plebiscites has limited and moderated the power of the CSU, which ruled alone for many years (Glaab, 2013). Popular legislation can thus provide a participation and decision-making procedure alternative to the parliamentary system. At the same time, it is also true: so far, direct democratic procedures have not been able to challenge the character of the governmental systems in the *Länder*. They were and are: parliamentary systems of government. The current challenges for the democratic systems in the *Länder* do not consist in an opposition between direct and representative procedures which is in any case constructed rather in terms of the history of ideas. Rather, the current problem seems to be that both participation procedures have a socially selective effect and are denied to be "of", "by" and "for the people". They exclude certain groups of residents (foreigners, children) and discriminate against less educated and socially precarious classes. These effects were particularly evident in the Hamburg referendum on school reform in 2010, in which members of the groups that would have benefited from the reform either participated little or—due to the lack of voting rights—not at all. But other studies also show that political participation is more socially selective in direct democratic procedures than in elections to parliaments (Bödeker, 2012; Merkel, 2011; Merkel & Petring, 2011). Overall, these findings allow the conclusion that the two procedures can be understood neither as opposites nor as complements. They are by no means mutually exclusive in constitutional practice. However, they also lack the potential to compensate for the deficits of the other procedure.

Parties and Party Systems in the *Länder*

5

Abstract

Democracy in Germany is party democracy. This basic principle of democratic theory also applies to the German *Länder*. The chapter therefore provides a systematic overview of the tasks and developments of parties and party systems in the 16 *Länder*. It also examines how *Land* parties and *Land* party systems relate to the federal level.

5.1   The Status of Parties in the *Länder*

According to Ludger Helms (2007b, p. 49), parties are "first and foremost" electoral "groups which, on the basis of common political convictions, strive to acquire the largest possible share of votes and mandates, usually in order to participate on this basis in the appointment of government offices". They are, therefore, associations of people who share similar political views, concerns and interests and who seek political office. They are situated between the state and society, are supposed to mediate between these two spheres, and are thus also "a reflection of the political interests and opinions held in society" (Schniewind, 2008a, p. 63). As in the federal government, the development of parties and party systems in the *Länder* is the result of elections and electoral systems (Helms, 2007b, p. 49).

Although parties perform key tasks for democracy in the *Länder*, they do not have a good reputation. In Saxony, just 12% of 1011 respondents in a 2018 survey said they trusted parties (Sachsen-Monitor, 2018, p. 24). Other surveys come to similar conclusions (Reiser et al., 2019, p. 41 f.). In liberal democratic systems, as they exist in the *Länder*, such findings can only be understood as alarm signals. After all, parliamentary democracies are party democracies, in which parties play an important, perhaps even the most important role. Ludger Helms (2007b, pp. 48–82) rightly describes parties in the Federal Republic of Germany as the "backbone of representative democracy". For this reason, parties have received recognition in the Basic Law that they were denied in the Constitution of the Weimar Republic. They are treated like "constitutional organs" (which they formally are not). According to Article 21 (1) and (2) of the Basic Law, parties can be freely founded and permanently maintained. Only the Federal Constitutional Court can ban a party if it seeks to impair or eliminate the "free democratic basic order" or endangers the "existence of the Federal Republic of Germany". Since 2017, the Federal Constitutional Court can also rule on whether a party can be excluded from public party funding.

The *Länder* have no powers in this area. They can neither ban nor permit parties. *Land* election committees can only decide whether a party meets the requirements to participate in *Land* elections. For example, on July 5, 2019, the Election Committee in Saxony refused to allow the AfD to run on two established electoral lists for the *Land* election on September 1, 2019. The Constitutional Court of Saxony, in its decisions of July 25, 2019 and August 16, 2019, partially re-allowed the electoral lists. The *Länder* can also participate in party prohibition proceedings via the *Bundesrat* (Federal Council) or apply to the Federal Constitutional Court to ban a party if that party is limited to the respective *Land*. No such application has been made to date. According to the Basic Law, the parties have only one task: they "participate in the formation of the political will of the people" (Article 21 (1) of the Basic Law). It must not be deduced from this that the parties have a monopoly in this respect. Of course, other persons or actors (such as associations, NGOs) may also participate in the formation of political will. Nor is this the only task that parties would have to fulfil. The "Law on Political Parties" (Parteiengesetz), which came into force in 1967, is more detailed in this respect. It states in Sect. 1 para. 2:

> "The parties shall participate in the formation of the political will of the people in all fields of public life, in particular by influencing the shaping of public opinion, by stimulating and deepening political education, by promoting the active participation of citizens in political life, by educating citizens capable of assuming public responsibility, by participating in federal, Land and municipal elections by nominating candidates, by influencing political developments in parliament and government, by introducing the political goals they have worked out into the process of forming the will of the state, and by ensuring a permanent living link between the people and the organs of the state."

The relevant research has attempted to sort out and evaluate the tasks that parties are supposed to fulfil from this rather confusing mix. In the debates on these issues, *Land* parties have for a long time "only played a marginal role" (Eilfort, 2006, p. 207), were "neglected" (Decker 2010, p. 91) or "paid little attention" to (Schneider, 1997, p. 407). This has changed. There are now quite a number of studies that focus on *Land* parties and *Land* party systems (Jun et al., 2008; Kost et al., 2010; Schniewind, 2012), not to mention introductory accounts of politics in *Länder* (Lorenz et al., 2016; Jesse et al., 2014; Glaab & Weigl, 2013; Träger & Priebus, 2017). The following analysis follows on from these studies and asks what significance parties and party systems have for the stability and functioning of democracies in the *Länder*. The assumption here is that parties in the *Länder* are not "mere offshoots or even 'command receivers'" of their federal counterparts (Leunig, 2012, p. 80). The idea that parties are centralized and hierarchically structured organizations, which has long dominated party research, is not shared. On the contrary, parties and party systems fulfil functions independently in the *Länder* and have an *independent* autonmous basis of legitimacy. Against this background, the tasks of *Land* parties are first described (Sect. 5.2); building on this, party systems are analyzed (Sect. 5.3; Decker, 2010; Haas et al., 2008, pp. 10–16; Eilfort, 2006; Schneider, 1997; Schniewind, 2012).

5.2   Tasks of Parties in the *Länder*

Parties have to fulfil the same tasks at federal and *Länder* level. In this, at least, research agrees (Eilfort, 2006, Schneider, 1997; Decker, 2010). Which tasks these are and how they are designated, however, is disputed (Jun, 2013; Niedermayer, 2013a). In the following, I follow Michael Eilfort (2006), for whom federal and *Land* parties do not differ "at first glance". But at second glance, Eilfort recognizes a whole range of differences, which he attributes to varying political frameworks, cultures, and so on. Eilfort distinguishes four areas of responsibility. It goes without saying that the parties in the *Länder* fulfil their tasks in varying ways. This depends, among other things, on election results, membership strength, role (governing or opposition party), self-image and the respective tradition (Jesse et al., 2014, pp. 161–186; Schneider, 1997; Kost et al., 2010).

(1) Mediation and representation function (Eilfort calls this: "transmission function"). Parties must represent the interests and concerns of their voters and represent them in the political and state decision-making process. In political science terminology this can be described as: Articulation, aggregation and representation of societal interests. This is a demanding task, especially for the so-called catch-all parties. For parties have to address different groups of voters in order to obtain as many votes as possible in elections. Parties must therefore take up the interests and concerns of different social groups in their programs, balance them and represent them vis-à-vis third parties. Michael Eilfort (2006, p. 209) argues that the smaller the parties' frame of reference, the easier it is for them to do this. In this respect, *Land* parties have an advantage over their federal counterparts: For parties in Hamburg or Bremen hardly have to champion agricultural concerns, while their sister organizations in Saarland or Rhineland-Palatinate are not pushed to champion maritime concerns. Federal parties, on the other hand, have to take up both issues and balance them. Eilfort (2006, p. 209) sees this as a productive "division of labor" because certain concerns can be vehemently advocated at the *Land* level, which can then be put into perspective at the federal level and embedded in "a larger whole."

(2) Socialization and mobilization function: Eilfort (2006, p. 210) considers the federal parties as "capable of making politics, but not viable and above all not ready for (election) campaigns." It is, in fact, the members of the *Land* parties and their subdivisions who stick posters, organize stalls in pedestrian zones or,

in short, run the election campaign on the ground. And this is by no means only true for *Land* elections, but also for elections to the *Bundestag* (Federal Diet) and the European Parliament. The socialization of office holders also usually but not always begins at the local level (Eilfort, 2006, p. 210). This refers to the notorious "oxen tour". In this variant, politicians rise successively. They pass through several committees at increasingly higher regional levels and are thus socialized into politics. In this respect, however, fundamental changes have taken place. For example, party membership numbers are continuously declining and also vary considerably (Niedermayer, 2019). In some *Länder*, the FDP, the Greens, the Left Party or even the SPD or CDU are not (or no longer) able to campaign nationwide and mobilize voters in the same way across the country.

(3) Recruitment function: According to Eilfort (2006, p. 211), *Land* parties have an "outstanding role" with regard to the recruitment function. It is they (together with the respective district and local branches) that provide the political personnel for municipal elective offices (mayors, local councilors), *Land* parliaments and government positions. Moreover, Eilfort (2006, p. 211) continues, "a large number of important federal politicians come from *Land* politics and have gained formative experience there in or as representatives of *Land* parties." In this context, Eilfort rightly points out that the chancellor and leading candidate of the respective largest opposition party were usually previously prime minister in a *Land* or chairperson of a *Land* party. Exceptions (such as Angela Merkel [CDU] in 2005 or Martin Schulz [SPD] in 2017) only confirm the rule. Sometimes, however, federal politicians take office at the *Land* level (for example, Manuela Schwesig [SPD] swapped her position as Federal Minister for Family Affairs with that of Minister President of Mecklenburg-Western Pomerania in 2017). In addition, a "careerization and professionalization of political personnel" is also taking place in *Länder* (Schneider, 1997, p. 419; see also Beyme, 1997a).

(4) Finally, the function of government-formation: Here the parties in the *Länder* fulfil the same tasks as in the federal government. They provide the personnel for the respective *Land* government and, if necessary, conclude a coalition agreement with one (or more) other party(ies) (Kropp, 2001; Kropp & Sturm, 1998; Jun, 1994). The laboratory function is particularly important in this context. New coalition constellations can be tested at the *Land* level, which can then be transferred to the federal level if necessary. In this respect, *Land* parties are not only a "reservoir of personnel" for the party system at the federal level, but also have an important "innovation potential" (Eilfort, 2006, p. 211).

5.3   Party Systems in the *Länder:* Structures and Development

A party system is more than the sum of its parts. It provides services that only become apparent when the network of relationships between the parts is included in the analysis and when the functions of the party system itself are taken into account (Helms, 1995; Haas et al., 2008; Niedermayer, 2013c). This also means that a distinction must be made between parties and party systems. For example: What may be interpreted as a crisis in a party may have no or even positive consequences for the party system. If, for example, the AfD were to disappear from parliaments again, this would be a crisis-like development for this party and its mandate holders, but not at all for the party system. This is immediately obvious. Nevertheless, this difference is often overlooked.

According to Aline Schniewind (2008a, p. 64), the field of *Land* party systems has so far been a rather step-motherly one. She also warns against equating *Land* party systems and federal party systems. Not only would these two be different, but also the *Land* party systems would have to be differentiated on the basis of their respective specific social structures, cultures and political traditions (Schniewind, 2008a, p. 64; Sturm, 2001, pp. 84–90). The remainder of this chapter follows on from this finding and asks how the party systems in the *Länder* have changed. However, it is not possible to present and compare the developments of the 16 *Land* party systems individually. This would far exceed the scope not only of this chapter but also of the book. Moreover, several overviews already exist that deal with *Land* parties and *Land* party systems (Schniewind, 2012; Leunig, 2012, pp. 76–104, Jun et al., 2008; Kost et al., 2010; Niedermayer, 2013c).

Changes in party systems can be described with different indicators. The most common one measures the number and strength of parties represented in parliament (Laakso & Taagepera, 1979). In addition, there are other indices such as concentration (= shares of SPD + CDU/CSU) or asymmetry (= vote shares of CDU/CSU—vote shares of SPD). Concentration gives an indication of the strength of the two—former—catch-all-parties. The indicator asymmetry describes the relationship between these two parties (Reutter, 2008, pp. 85–87; Niedermayer, 1996, p. 24). The index of integration gives an indication of the proportion of voters who are effectively represented in parliament.

The following analysis aims to discuss general developments by means of an "asymmetrical comparison" (Kocka, 1999). In concrete terms, this means that the "case" of Berlin will be used to work out the common features and special characteristics of party systems in the *Länder* after 1946 (Table 5.1).[1] A distinction is made between four phases of development: The constitutional phase between 1945 and 1949 (1) was followed by a period of stabilization and concentration until the end of the 1970s, which came to an end with the founding of the Green Party (2). Retrospectively, the 1980s were to prove to be a kind of transformation phase (3), which was steered into new directions by unification (4).

(1) Constitution (1945–1949): After the unconditional surrender on May 8, 1945, parties had to be newly founded (Sect. 2.1). Such a founding act was always subject to approval by the Allies. The forerunner in this phase was the Soviet occupying authority known as SMAD, which permitted the founding of

---

[1]In the following, I draw on Reutter (2012), pp. 151–155 as well as Reutter (2008), pp. 84–96; See for Berlin also: Lempp (2010), Reichart-Dreyer (2008); Massing (1990) and Rytlewski (1999).

Table 5.1 Development of Berlin's party system (1950–2016) (See explanations in the text). (*Sources* Reutter, 2012, p. 152; Statistisches Landesamt Berlin, 2006 ff., own additions and calculations)

Election Year	Parties running for election	Parties in Parliament	Fragmentation	Integration	Concentration (CDU + SPD)	Asymmetry (CDU-SPD)	Proportion of right-wing extremist/populist parties
	(abs.)	(abs.)	(N)	(%)	(%)		(%)
1950	8	3	3.2	81.3	69.4	−20.0	–
1954	9	3	3.2	79.6	75.0	−14.2	–
1958	6	2	2.4	86.5	90.3	−14.9	–
1963	4	3	2.1	87.7	90.7	−33.1	–
1967	5	3	2.3	72.3	89.8	−24.0	–
1971	5	3	2.5	85.1	88.6	−12.2	–
1975	7	3	2.6	81.4	86.5	+1.3	–
1979	6	3	2.6	79.7	87.1	+1.7	–
1981	6	4	2.6	82.5	86.3	+9.7	–
1985	9	4	2.9	80.8	78.8	+14.0	–
1989	10	4	3.3	71.1	75.0	+0.4	7.5
1990	10	5	3.6	77.1	70.8	+10.0	3.1
1995	19	4	4.2	61.5	61.0	+13.8	2.7
1999	17	4	3.8	60.2	63.2	+18.4	3.5
2001	14	5	4.7	63.8	53.5	−5.9	2.2
2006	23	5	5.0	49.0	52.1	−8.5	3.5
2011	22	5	5.3	53.1	51.5	−4.9	2.1
2016	21	6	6.5	59.8	39.2	−4.0	14.8

"anti-fascist parties" as early as June 10, 1945. The military administrations of the Western zones followed suit a little later (Leunig, 2012, pp. 80–86). In Berlin, the founding phase of the parties was also marked by an intensifying East—West conflict. This reached its dramatic climax in the forced unification of the Communist Party with the Social Democratic Party of Germany, which was restricted to the eastern part of the city and supported there by the Soviet occupying power (Massing, 1990, p. 154). In the other *Länder* of the Federal Republic, the formation phase from 1946 to 1949 was also marked by the founding of new parties. Due to the licensing policy of the Allies, the number of parties remained limited in all *Länder* until 1949. Party building took place from the bottom up.

(2) Concentration, stability, integration (1949–1977): The phase after the adoption of the Basic Law until the end of the 1970s can be described with the three keywords mentioned above (Leunig, 2012, pp. 86–98). Once again, the Berlin case has some peculiarities (Rytlewski, 1999; Reutter, 2012; Reichart-Dreyer, 2008). The first election to the Berlin House of Representatives was characterized by the described antecedents. The KPD did not play a role here—in contrast to other *Länder*. Its successor organizations (SED, SED-W and SEW) also never managed to enter the House of Representatives of Berlin. The SPD and CDU received up to 90% of the vote in Berlin; on average, six parties stood for election, half of which entered parliament; accordingly, the number of effective parties fell to as few as 2.1. This corresponds to the high proportion of eligible voters who were effectively represented in the House of Representatives because they had voted for a party that managed to enter parliament (integration). During this period, party competition in Berlin and in the other *Länder* functioned as in a two-party system. Two large catch-all-parties and one small party competed for voters. In Berlin, the SPD dominated, providing the head of government almost continuously until 1981.[2] This social democratic "hegemony" (Rytlewski, 1999, p. 320) made the SPD appear as *the* Berlin party par excellence.

Similar developments took place in the other *Länder*, albeit under different circumstances. In the southern *Länder* (Bavaria and Baden-Württemberg), for example, the CSU and CDU were particularly strong, while the SPD was able to achieve successes in the city states and in northern *Länder* (Reutter, 2008, pp. 88 f.; Weichlein, 2019, pp. 118–153; Sturm, 2001, pp. 84–90). In the 40 *Land* elections held between 1946 and 1961, about 76% of eligible voters participated, with the major parties, the CDU, CSU, and SPD, receiving an average of about 70% of the votes cast. Polarization was low, even though the far-right NPD was represented in several *Land* parliaments (and still managed to garner 4.3% of the second votes in the 1969 federal election). It is also noteworthy that in the *Länder* the SPD did better than the conservative parties, while in federal elections the CDU/CSU regularly received the most votes.

---

[2]Walther Schreiber (CDU) was Governing Mayor of Berlin for two years after the death of Ernst Reuter (SPD) in 1953.

(3) Transformation (1977–1990): In the 1980s, the party systems in the *Länder* and in Berlin underwent a fundamental transformation, which, however, unfolded itself in different ways and exhibited *Land*-specific characteristics in each case. In Berlin, from 1977 onwards, a power shift took place in favour of the CDU, which became the strongest party and eventually assumed government responsibility (Rytlewski, 1999, pp. 321–325; Reutter, 2012, pp. 153–154). At the same time, the number of parties participating in elections to the Berlin House of Representatives or even entering the Berlin parliament increased. The Alternative List for Democracy and Environmental Protection (*Alternative Liste für Demokratie und Umweltschutz*, AL)—the Berlin offshoot of the Green Party founded in 1977— succeeded in 1981, and the right-wing populist Republicans (*"Republikaner"*) in 1989 (Massing, 1990, pp. 160–161). During this period, the SPD and CDU were only able to garner an average of 75% of the votes cast. Nevertheless, the change of government in 1989 came as a surprise to most. Although the CDU remained the strongest party in this election despite considerable losses, a grand coalition had been ruled out by both the SPD and the CDU before the election. The only possible option was thus the first red-green coalition in Berlin. What had begun in 1977 with the founding of the AL, continued in 1979 with its first participation in the elections and in 1981 with its entry into the House of Representatives, led to government participation in 1989. But the Red-Green government under Walter Momper (SPD) as Governing Mayor remained short-lived. The coalition ended already on November 19, 1990, even before the new elections, which had been brought forward anyway, with the resignation of the three AL senators.

A comparison of the development in Berlin with that in the other *Länder* once again brings out peculiarities and commonalities. The Green Party or its respective branches in the *Länder* began to participate in elections and successively started to enter *Land* parliaments in 1977. For other parties, this was apparently motivation enough to also run for parliamentary mandates. Voter turnout in the *Länder* was still exceptionally high during this period, almost reaching the 80% mark on average. The catch-all-parties did not yet need to worry too much, as they accounted for an average of around 86% of the votes cast (Reutter, 2008, pp. 89–97).

(4) With unification, the party systems in the *Länder* underwent another fundamental change (Niedermayer, 1997). The Berlin case is representative here: On the one hand, the long-term trends that had already become apparent in the 1980s intensified. There were even more parties (fragmentation), the two major parties lost votes (concentration), and the parties in parliament represented fewer voters (integration). On the other hand, new structures emerged in Berlin. The formerly highly concentrated party system with two large catch-all-parties has been transformed into a multipolar system without a political center of gravity. The number of effective parties rose to over six in the last election; the CDU and SPD together were able to claim just 39% of the votes cast in the 2016 election (which corresponded to 25.8% of eligible voters). In addition, with the AfD, a decidedly right-wing populist, in parts even right-wing extremist party, succeeded in entering the House of Representatives, and it appears that voting behavior in the eastern part of the city differs significantly from that in the western part. Similar developments

took place in the other *Länder*. There, too, the age of the catch-all-parties is gradually coming to an end. With significantly lower voter turnout, the CDU/CSU and SPD in the *Länder* are less and less able to bind voters to themselves, which makes it more difficult to form a government. At the same time, parties on the left and right fringes of the political spectrum have gained in weight and importance. The coalition landscape is now correspondingly colourful.

Notwithstanding the seemingly parallel developments, the analysis of elections and party systems in the *Länder* paints a mixed picture. In his analysis of the *Land* party systems, Oskar Niedermayer concludes that one should be "very careful with generalizing statements" about similarities or differences (Niedermayer, 2013c, p. 782). The *Land* party systems vary so much that one cannot speak of "homogeneity". Even longer-term developments do not reveal any systematic differences that would justify, according to Niedermayer, "clearly distinguishing between different groups of *Länder*, not even between the east and west Germans" (Niedermayer, 2013c, p. 782).

Keeping this in mind, the findings presented here allow for three conclusions: First, party competition and party systems have become more complex since unification. Former political strongholds have disappeared. The decades-long supremacy of the CDU in Baden-Württemberg is history. The same applies to the SPD in Brandenburg and Bremen, to the CDU in Saxony and Thuringia. Only the CSU can still reasonably hope to remain the dominant party in Bavaria for the foreseeable future. Secondly, one cannot speak of a "decoupling" of the party systems of the federal and *Land* governments. Nevertheless, there is much evidence pointing to a pronounced tendency towards regionalization (Hough & Jeffery, 2003; Sturm, 2001, pp. 81–90; Niedermayer, 1997; Detterbeck & Renzsch, 2008; Detterbeck, 2019; Decker & Blumenthal, 2002). The *Länder* play an increasingly important and autonomous role for parties and for party competition. Third, small parties have repeatedly succeeded in entering *Land* parliaments. This applies not only to the Green party or their respective regional variants such as the GAL in Hamburg or the AL in Berlin but also to right-wing populist or right-wing extremist parties such as the NPD, the Republicans, the DVU, the Schill Party, the AfD and other splinter groups. The Free Voters (Freie Wähler) are now also represented in parliament in Bavaria and Brandenburg. In the party systems of the *Länder*, therefore, more and different things happen than in the federal government. In this respect, they deserve an independent role for democracy in the Federal Republic of Germany.

Parliaments, Governments and Constitutional Courts: Division of Powers in the *Länder*

6

Abstract

Governing in the *Länder* is similar to governing at the federal level—and yet different. Like the federal government, *Land* governments are dependent on the respective parliament and can be controlled by the courts. However, unlike at the federal level, there are no second chambers of parliament in the *Länder* and unlike at the federal level, *Land* constitutional courts have so far not been able to attain anywhere near the importance of the Federal Constitutional Court at the central state level. The chapter describes principles of the separation of powers in the *Länder* as well as the structure, functioning and significance of *Land* parliaments, *Land* governments, and *Land* constitutional courts.

6.1 Division of Powers in the *Länder*

Although not the first, Montesquieu was by far the most influential theoretician to deal with the question of how a state should be built in order to secure the freedom of its citizens (Oberreuter, 1992b; Schmidt, 2000, pp. 74–90). In the famous 6th chapter of the XIth book of his main work "The Spirit of Laws" (*De l'esprit des lois*), published in 1748, Charles-Louis de Secondat, Baron de La Brède de Montesquieu, as he was called by his full name, describes the "Constitution of England" and derives general principles from it. These principles are still valid today. Montesquieu (1979)[1] defines in this chapter three public powers: the legislative, the executive and the judiciary. To prevent the abuse of public power and to

---

[1] The translation is from the edition published by the Online Library of Liberty; https://oll.libertyfund.org/title/montesquieu-complete-works-vol-1-the-spirit-of-laws (accessed: December 7, 2020).

guarantee freedom, it is imperative "from the very nature of things" to ensure that "power should be a check to power (Book XI, Chap. 4), or "le pouvoir arrête le pouvoir" in the original. Thus, Montesquieu does not believe in the virtue of man. He rather assumes that even "virtue itself has need of limits" (Book XI, Chap. 4). And these limits can be marked by a certain "arrangement of things" or by a system of "checks and balances". The "arrangement of things" can now be done in different ways.

In the German *Länder*, the division of legislative, executive and judicial powers functions similarly to that of the Federation–but under different conditions. As in the Basic Law, the separation of powers is a basic principle of constitutional law in the *Länder*. The state functions of legislation, execution and jurisdiction are exercised by the organs mentioned in the constitutions. As in the Federation, the Federal Government, in the *Länder* the *Land* governments are dependent on the respective parliament, and are of course bound by the Constitution and by law. Administrative and constitutional courts can control this in case of doubt and oblige parliament and government to observe the law. However, unlike at federal level, there are no second "chambers of parliament" in the *Länder* and unlike at federal level, the constitutional courts of *Länder* have not yet been able to achieve anywhere near the importance of the Federal Constitutional Court at central government level. The possibility of popular legislation and other direct democratic procedures in *Länder*, which have so far been of no significance at federal level, has been mentioned, as well. All this must be taken into account when the structures, working methods and role of the three constitutional bodies mentioned above, as well as their relationship to each other, are described below.

6.2   *Land* Parliaments: The Legislative Power

Parliaments and democracy belong together in the *Länder*. This makes the widely held view that *Land* parliaments have continuously lost power and influence all the more dramatic (Eicher, 1988; Thaysen, 2005). For Hans-Herbert von Arnim, they have even already been abolished—in "light of day" —and are now only "nesting holes" for the "political class", which, according to Arnim, wants to secure parliamentary mandates and "other "benefactors" (Arnim, 2002, pp. 162 f.; see also Kirbach, 2002). Such distorted images have nothing to do with parliamentary reality (Reutter, 2008, pp. 349–341; Carstensen & Schüttemeyer, 2015; Jesse et al., 2014, p. 69). Rather and as Werner J. Patzelt (2006, p. 128) assumes, *Land* parliaments provide an additional level of "political responsiveness", co-governance, and political leadership. They are thus democratic representative bodies that pass laws and form and control governments. In addition, "blanket judgements" are impossible to make and lead to nothing (Jesse et al., 2014, p. 72). The structures, working methods and functions of the people's representative bodies vary between *Länder*, as the further description makes clear.

6.2.1 Structure and Mode of Operation

For historical reasons, the parliaments in the *Flächenländer* (area states) are called "Landtag" ("state parliament"), in Berlin "Abgeordnetenhaus" ("House of Representatives") and in Bremen and Hamburg "Bürgerschaft" ("Citizenry"). At the end of December 2019, these parliaments counted in sum 1866 members, with Saarland having 51 and Bavaria 205. Mathematically, one member of parliament in Bremen thus represented 5661 eligible voters in 2019, compared with 72,734 in North Rhine-Westphalia. The members of parliament are not bound by any orders or instructions in any parliament. They are subject only to their conscience and always represent the respective people of the *Land* as a whole (and not just their constituency or party).

No parliament in the world can map the social structure one to one. Nor does it have to. Rather, it must be able to accommodate the various social interests and concerns, or in Patzelt's words: it must be "responsive". From a sociological point of view, the *Land* parliaments also have some prerequisites for this. The members of parliament differ according to origin, education, profession, age and gender. According to respective studies, however, the professional politician who lives "from" politics now dominates in the *Land* parliaments. These politicians draw their income, called diets, from their profession as a member of parliament. His/her tasks consist mainly of "meetings" and information and contact activities. At least these are the results of surveys among members of parliament (Patzelt, 1995; Reutter, 2008, p. 138; Schüttemeyer et al., 1999). Moreover: In 2013 a *Land* parliament cost each citizen on average of only about 15 euros per year (Reutter, 2013, p. 22).

Structurally, *Land* parliaments can be described with three terms: They are constitutional organs, a mixture of a speech and working parliament as well as factional parliaments (see also Reutter, 2008, pp. 149–192; Leunig, 2012, 61–158; Leunig & Reutter, 2012; Carstensen & Schüttemeyer, 2015).

- As a "constitutional body", the *Land* parliaments are entitled to regulate their internal affairs themselves. They have their own section in the *Land* budget, and their functions are at least partially defined in the Constitution. All *Land* parliaments have adopted rules of procedure. They elect their governing bodies themselves, which usually consist of a president, one or more vice-presidents, a presidium, a council of elders and recording clerks. These bodies may have different names in the parliaments. They represent parliament to the outside world, ensure internal order and ensure that parliamentary business runs as smoothly as possible. As a rule, all the political groups are represented on these bodies, because this is the only way to ensure parliamentary workflows. However, the entry of the AfD into the *Land* parliaments has led to conflicts in this respect (Reutter, 2016a). The role of the presidents is particularly noteworthy. As a rule, they belong to the strongest parliamentary group and are difficult or impossible to remove from office. They (or, if applicable, vice presidents) have far-reaching powers: They represent the parliament externally, exercise authority in parliament, chair plenary sessions, are the highest hierarchical superiors of the parliamentary administrations, draw up the budgets and, finally, perform tasks which the head of state performs at the federal level (e.g. certification and promulgation of laws).

- "Working and speech parliaments": This pair of terms refers to different functions, but it is also expressed in parliamentary bodies, namely in the plenary and in the specialist committees. In most cases, a parliament is equated with the plenum, i.e. the assembly of the members of parliament. The half-empty plenary hall, which is often shown on television, is then regarded as proof that the members of parliament are not doing their job. However, this is a misperception. For in "working parliaments"—as the *Land* parliaments are above all—committees play a central role. Specialist committees are auxiliary organs of the plenum and are supposed to prepare its resolutions. In parliamentary practice, their influence goes even further. They discuss and amend draft laws and control the government, and are therefore not only auxiliary bodies, but often anticipate decisions of the plenum. They also meet much more frequently than the plenary assemblies (Reutter, 2013, p. 26). *Land* parliaments have several specialist committees (in 2006 the average number was 12; Reutter, 2013, p. 26), whose content is geared—more or less—to the departments of the respective *Land* government. This makes it easier for the committees to monitor the executive branch and to discuss legislative proposals. At the same time, it expresses the close interlocking of parliamentary work with the government. In addition, *Land* parliaments can establish committees of inquiry and commissions of enquiry. In Bremen and Hamburg, there are also "deputations" that monitor the administration. Final decisions on laws can only be made in plenary sessions, which are usually convened at regular intervals by the respective president after a well-established practice. For example, the Landtag of Brandenburg meets approximately every four weeks from Wednesday to Thursday or Friday; in Berlin the plenum meets every two weeks for one day. It goes without saying that these rules can be deviated from at any time. The course of a plenary session is meticulously planned. There is little room for surprises, which of course occur time and again.

- The term "factional parliament" refers to the pivotal role parliamentary groups play in these bodies. Parliamentary systems of government are unthinkable without (parties and) parliamentary groups. They would just not function. Factions are legally responsible associations of members of parliament who usually belong to the same party. Factions or parliamentary groups are founded at the beginning of a legislative term by a minimum number of members of parliament (e.g. 5%). If this minimum number is not reached, members of parliament may form a parliamentary group or exercise their mandate independently and individually. Parliamentary groups are entitled to the most important parliamentary rights. Sven Leunig (2012, p. 146) correctly emphasized that the concentration of parliamentary prerogatives on the parliamentary groups indicates not only their importance, but also the degree of "mediatization" of the individual member of parliament, who can participate in many parliamentary functions only via the parliamentary group he or she belongs to. Like the *Land* parliaments as a whole, the parliamentary groups also adopt rules of procedure to regulate their internal affairs (Reutter, 2008, pp. 183–192). Depending on their size, the parliamentary groups all have similar structures (group chairman/ chairwoman, executive committee, working groups, parliamentary director) and functional principles. It would be a misunderstanding to see a contradiction between parliamentary groups and group discipline on the one hand and the free mandate of members of parliament on the other (Patzelt, 1998b). On the contrary, the two are interdependent and conditional on each other. A single member of parliament would be hopelessly overtaxed and remain without influence on parliamentary events if he/she did not join forces with others. That is why he—or she—is dependent on the group community. At the same time, only members of parliament have the most important resource in parliament: the right to vote (Patzelt, 1998b; Reutter, 2008, pp. 183–192).

In this structure, based on the division of labor, parliamentary decision-making takes place. It is the basis and prerequisite for *Land* parliaments to be able to fulfil their tasks.

6.2.2 Tasks: "Talking and Acting"[2]

Classification and evaluation of parliamentary performance depends on how parliaments are understood. If one understands parliaments primarily as a place of public debate on political issues (Habermas, 1993; Schmitt, 1988), one will examine parliamentary debates that take place in the plenary assembly of parliamentarians. If one believes that a parliament is primarily responsible for enacting laws and controlling the government, the committees are in the foreground. Four functions are described in more detail below, following Walter Bagehot (1993). This is intended to give as comprehensive a picture as possible of the *Land* parliamentary functions (for further details see: Reutter, 2008, pp. 193–310; Leunig & Reutter, 2012; Carstensen & Schüttemeyer, 2015).

Creative function (elective function): Like the *Bundestag* (Federal Diet), *Land* parliaments elect members of other constitutional or *Land* organs and other bodies. These include the heads of government, constitutional judges, members of *Land* broadcasting councils or members of the Federal Assembly, which in turn elects the Federal President. The list could easily be extended. In most cases, these elections take place as smoothly and quietly as possible. But not always. Recently, many elections of parliamentary presidents or committee chairmen have posed a challenge (Reutter, 2016a, p. 607). The effective fulfilment of the elective

---

[2]I borrow this characterization from Carstensen and Schüttemeyer (2015).

Table 6.1 Election of heads of government in the German Länder (*Source* Klecha (2010, pp. 209, 215, 213), Reutter (2013, p. 50); Pestalozza (2014b); own additions)

State	First ballot majority	Relative majority (later ballot)	Time frame[a]	Parliamentary dissolution in case of failure[c]	Vote of no confidence[b]	Vote of confidence
BW	Absolute	No	3 months	Yes	Constructive	No
BAV	Simple	Yes	1 week	No	Simple	No
BER	Absolute	Yes	None	No	Simple	No
BB	Absolute	Yes	3 months	Yes	Constructive	Yes
BRE	Simple	Yes	None	No	Constructive	No
HAM	Absolute	No	None	No	Constructive	Yes
HES	Absolute	No	None	No	Simple	No
MW	Absolute	Yes	4 weeks	Possible	Constructive	Yes
LS	Absolute	Yes	3 weeks	Possible	Constructive	No
NRW	Absolute	Yes	None	No	Constructive	No
RP	Absolute	No	None	No	Simple	No
SLD	Absolute	No	3 months	Yes	Simple	Yes
SAY	Absolute	Yes	4 months	Yes	Constructive	No
SAT	Absolute	Yes	2 weeks	Possible	Constructive	Yes
SH	Absolute	Yes	None	No	Constructive	Yes
TH	Absolute	Yes	None	No	Constructive	Yes

[a]after the meeting of a newly elected *Land* parliament
[b]in Bavaria, the minister president must resign if cooperation based on trust is no longer possible; in Berlin, the vote of no confidence lapses if no new head of government is elected within three weeks; in Hesse, Rhineland-Palatinate and Saarland, a new government must be appointed within twelve days, four weeks and three months respectively, otherwise the *Landtag* is dissolved
[c]in MW and LS, a parliamentary resolution is necessary; in principle, all *Land* parliaments have the possibility of self-dissolution

function is therefore not a given and depends on the party-political majority in the respective *Land* parliament.

With Schneider (2001, p. 13; March 2006), the election of heads of government can be understood as a "quasi-plebiscitary" act of legitimation. This is because the parties compete in elections with top candidates who claim the post of head of government if they successfully complete the elections. To this extent, in the election of the prime minister, the parliament usually "ratifies" only the election result (Anter & Frick, 2016, p. 106). As mentioned above, things get complicated if the elections do not result in a clear majority and the parliament does not succeed in electing a head of government. It is then not possible to form a government. In this case, either the old government remains in office or the parliament is dissolved.

Nevertheless, the election of a head of government is regarded as the "heart of the parliamentary system of government of German character" (Neumann, 2000, p. 198). However, this "heart" does not always beat in the parliaments at the same rhythm (Klecha, 2010; Ley, 2010, 2015, 2016; Leunig, 2012, pp. 179–200). This affects all aspects of the electoral act (Table 6.1):

- Majority: In most state parliaments, an absolute majority, i.e. more than 50% of the elected representatives, is necessary to put a head of government in office. In others (BAV and BRE) a majority of the votes cast is sufficient. In five *Länder* a minority government is possible, in the others not.
- Time frame: In some *Land* parliaments, a head of government must be elected within a certain period of time after a legislative period has started; in others, the old government remains in office until a majority has been found to form a government. In some cases, failure to install a new government leads to the dissolution of parliament, while in others this consequence is not obligatory.
- Vote of no-confidence/vote of confidence: In five *Länder* the parliament can bring down the government with a simple vote of no confidence, in others—as in the Bundestag–this is only possible by electing a new head of government. After all, only in six *Länder* the heads of government can ask for a vote of confidence (Reutter, 2005).

Irrespective of the variations mentioned, it is difficult to speak of functional deficits or functional problems in this area. In any case, there is no indication whatsoever that *Land* parliaments have lost power in forming a government. The parliaments were able to perform this task efficiently (naturally on the basis of election results and party agreements). *Land* governments came into office quickly and usually with stable majorities. Votes of no confidence were just as rare as self-dissolutions of parliaments, not to mention minority governments, which remained rare exceptions and can usually only be regarded as transitional phenomena (Reutter, 2008, pp. 208–230; Klecha, 2010; Leunig, 2017). However, in recent years the election results have made the conditions for forming a government in the *Länder* considerably more difficult, which is reflected not only in the length of time it takes to install a government but also in the fact that coalitions must be formed between parties that have little in common politically. This was particularly dramatic in Thuringia, where Thomas Kemmerich (FDP) was elected minister-president by the *Landtag* on February 5, 2020 with the votes of the CDU, FDP and AfD. In the third round of voting, he received one vote more than his rival candidate Bodo Ramelow (Left Party). It was not possible to form a government on this basis. Kemmerich did not appoint any ministers, was therefore unable to set up a cabinet, and resigned from office just three days later, on February 8, 2020. Kemmerich's election was rightly qualified as a "breach of taboo". For it was the first time in the history of the Federal Republic of Germany that a head of government was elected to his office with the support of a right-wing extremist party.

Legislative function: Laws are the state's most important medium for steering and shaping the society, and through legislation parliaments fulfil their task of

actively participating in governing (Oberreuter, 1992a). At this point it is not possible to go into whether and to what extent the laws passed have led to the desired
effects, and what the causes for individual legislative projects were. Such questions are answered in the context of policy analyses or in the context of legislative
studies (Beyme, 1997b; Hildebrandt & Wolf, 2016b). Here it can only be a matter
of outlining the legislative activity of the *Land* parliaments. Three aspects are of
importance here.

Firstly, unlike at federal level, there is only one constitutional body in the
Länder that can make final decisions on draft laws: the *Land* parliament. (The people are not a constitutional organ.) Different majority ratios in two legislative bodies are not possible in the *Länder*. There are no second chambers or other bodies
in the *Länder* whose consent would be required to bring a law into force.[3] From
the perspective of democratic theory, this is undoubtedly an advantage because
policy results can be clearly attributed and are achieved transparently (Fig. 6.1).

Laws are the rules that are "adopted as laws by the legislator in procedures provided for this purpose" (Hesse & Ellwein, 2012, p. 363). This definition refers to
the fact that what a law is cannot be deduced from its content, but only from the
applied procedure. Legislative procedures must meet democratic requirements
(Beyme, 1999, p. 282; Reutter, 2008, p. 231; Oberreuter, 1992a). This applies to
all stages of the legislative process in the *Land* parliaments. In all *Länder*, governments, parliamentary groups and the people can introduce bills in the *Land* parliament. In some *Land* parliaments, individual members of parliament (e.g., BW,
SLD) can also do so; in Brandenburg, even the president, the presidium, or permanent committees can do so (Fig. 6.1). In some *Land* parliaments, a bill can be
rejected in the first reading (e.g., in BB and NRW); in others, referral to a committee is mandatory (LS or SAT). Committees can meet in public or in closed session. And finally, in most *Land* parliaments, a final decision can be made on a draft
at second reading. In these cases, a third reading only takes place upon request
(e.g. BB) or in the case of budget laws and laws that change the constitution. In
most *Länder*, the head of government (minister president or mayor) has to prom-
ulgate any law. In five *Länder* (BER, BB, LS, SAY, TH) this task is assigned to
the President of the Landtag, in Bremen and Hamburg to the Senate. (Sometimes
participating ministers or prime ministers have to countersign).

The widely shared assumption that *Land* parliaments are continuously losing
power and influence is based primarily on the hypothesis that the number and quality of laws are declining. In this perspective, *Land* parliaments pass fewer and only
unimportant laws. However, the question of what constitutes a "satisfactory output of
laws" (Beyme, 1999, p. 282) can hardly be answered. After all, it can be stated that
between 1946 and 2009 the Hessian *Land* parliament passed an average of 101 laws
per year, while in Thuringia it averaged 147 between 1990 and 2009, i.e. almost 50%
more. Nor has the number of laws passed fallen continuously over time. From the

---

[3]The Senate, which existed in Bavaria until 1999, only had a suspensive veto right over legislative decisions of the Land parliament. It remained ineffective until its abolition.

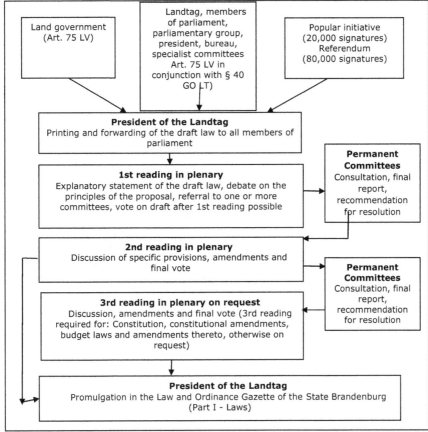

(Source: according to Brandenburger Landtag 2010, p. 176)

Fig. 6.1 Legislative process in Brandenburg (as of 2010). (*Source* According to Brandenburger Landtag, 2010, p. 176)

beginning of the 1990s onwards, one can even speak of a "legislative renaissance", because after German unification, a particularly large number of laws were passed in the west and east German *Länder* (Reutter, 2008, pp. 238–249). Similarly, the assumption that *Land* parliaments would at best pass implementing and adaptation laws could not be confirmed in studies. Reus and Vogel (2018, p. 640) also show that the reform of the federal system, by which in the year 2006 a number of legislative powers were transferred to the *Länder*, has led to "substantial policy diversity". By this they mean that in the 15 policy areas they examined the *Länder* have adopted different regulations. Töller and Roßegger (2018) come to similar conclusions in their study on deviation legislation. In short, *Land* parliaments continue to perform legislative tasks.

Parliamentary control: In principle, a parliament should be able to monitor the use of state power by the government and administration. This is the democratic quality of parliamentary control. Only if it functions effectively, voters can make informed decisions (Möllers, 2008; Holtmann, 2007, Reutter, 2008, pp. 256–292). Accordingly, the *Land* parliaments take this task very seriously. However, it is not entirely clear who controls whom in parliamentary government systems, "and with what effect" (Holtmann et al., 2004). Does the parliament control the government, or does the government control the parliament? And as with legislation, the answers in the relevant political science studies differ. They essentially depend on how control is understood. Conceptually, there are two possibilities. The first: Usually the concept of control is limited to the retrospective scrutiny of governmental and administrative actions. This task is generally assigned to parties in opposition, which uses the appropriate instruments to do so. It obtains the necessary information by means of small, large and written questions, and question times, or sets up committees of inquiry and commissions of enquiry. It also tries to publicly address the problems and deficits of the incumbent government in plenary debates or topical issues. This happens with varying frequency in *Land* parliaments and often with unclear success. Nevertheless, long-term developments indicate that the above-mentioned means of control are being used more frequently. Whether, and to what extent, such control activities bring the opposition closer to its ultimate goal of ousting and replacing the government can at best be claimed for spectacular individual cases, but otherwise is difficult to prove. In addition, there is an insoluble dilemma for the opposition. For through its activities, it contributes to improving government and administrative actions. On the other hand: For the second form of control the term "parliamentary co-control" (parlamentarische Mitsteuerung) has become established (Schwarzmeier, 2001). This consists in the fact that the parliamentary majority usually participates informally in governmental activities. Karin Algasinger, Jürgen von Oertzen and Helmar Schöne (2004) found in their study that the Saxon *Land* parliament "fully and completely fulfilled" its task of controlling the government. Anyone who believes that parliament cannot control the government, or even thinks that the government controls parliament, is mistaken (Algasinger et al., 2004, p. 146).

Expressive/informing function (communication, representation, and articulation): The public sphere is an elementary component of democratic politics. For some theorists, parliamentarism even merges with public debate (Habermas, 1993; Schmitt, 1988). Consequently, this principle also applies to *Land* parliaments. In any case, constitutional law stipulates that *Land* parliaments should debate in public (e.g. Article 33 of the Constitution of Baden-Württemberg or Article 22 of the Bavarian Constitution). The expressive or informing function is therefore an essential task. Behind this idea we often find the somewhat naïve consideration that the members of parliament form their will in parliamentary debate, through public, enlightening negotiations, through argument and counter-argument, and come to a proper decision. This principle is put into practice by making plenary debates public, by taking minutes of them and by making the minutes available to all. More importantly, the parliamentary requirement for transparency is supplemented by the fact that the media can report freely on plenary events.

It goes without saying that the practical requirement for transparency in parliament is far removed from the theoretical considerations mentioned above. The parliamentary general will, i.e. the parliamentary decision, is at best exceptionally formed solely on the basis of the "forceless force" of the better argument generated in a plenary debate, as Jürgen Habermas (1991, p. 123) once formulated in another context. Plenary debates were rather, critics argue, nothing more than a collection of window-dressing speeches. Moreover, the topics were only rarely of interest to the extra-parliamentary public. Uwe Jun (1993, p. 502), therefore comes to the sobering conclusion that the communication function of state parliaments is "de facto only insufficiently perceived." In addition, the work of the *Land* parliaments largely eludes mass media communication. The functional logic of mass media makes it almost impossible to draw a realistic picture of parliamentary processes and procedures (Oberreuter, 1996; Marschall, 1999). This may also be the reason why knowledge of the functional principles of parliamentary government systems does not seem to be very widespread among citizens (Patzelt, 1998a, 1998b).

6.3   *Land* Governments and *Land* Administrations: The Executive Power

In some *Land* constitutions, *Land* governments are referred to as the "supreme body of executive power" (e.g. in Article 64 (1) of the Constitution of Saxony). In this perspective, it is the responsibility of *Land* governments to implement the laws passed by parliament. In constitutional reality, however, the remit of *Land* governments is broader. In general, it consists of directing and guiding the political communities of a *Land* (Schniewind, 2008b, p. 111). Or as it says on the homepage of the *Land* government of Baden-Württemberg: "The government directs the fate of the *Land*" (https://www.baden-wuerttemberg.de/de/regierung/landesregierung/). This is a task that is as demanding as it is complex, and which *Land* governments have sometimes solved more, sometimes less successfully (Jesse et al., 2014, pp. 93–136; Anter & Frick, 2016; Leunig, 2017; Glaab & Weigl, 2013). In this chapter, first the constitutional foundations and then central areas of responsibility of *Land* governments are presented.

6.3.1   Structure and Mode of Operation

Land governments, which are called "Senate" in Berlin, Hamburg and Bremen and "State Government" in Bavaria, Saxony and Thuringia, are independent constitutional bodies. Their composition and competences are regulated in the constitution and they have the right, in some cases even the duty, to adopt rules of procedure (e.g. Art. 53 of the constitution of Bavaria). In conjunction with the constitutional provisions, the rules of procedure lay down how the government functions and how it is to conduct government business. At the same time, *Land* governments depend on *Land* parliaments. They are part of parliamentary systems of government, which are formally distinguished by the fact that the head of government can be voted out of office by parliament (Steffani, 1979). This is based on a specific understanding of the separation of powers. The government and parliament are independent constitutional bodies in parliamentary systems of government. In functional terms, however, they depend on each other. For the government this means that the head of government as described above must be elected by parliament, or at least he/she depends on the trust of a parliamentary majority, as is the case with the entire government (Leunig, 2012, pp. 158–166; Reutter 2008, pp. 194–199). The term "new dualism" has become established to capture this interdependence. Whereas in the "old dualism", parliament and government face each other as institutions, in the "new dualism", government and parliamentary government majority form a functional unit. However, *Land* governments are not mere committees of parliament. Rather, they are constitutionally endowed with a "core area of executive autonomy". This covers the processes of decision-making by the government, which are beyond parliamentary control.

That was the theory. In government practice there are many variations and deviations from the principles mentioned above. This starts with the process of government formation. Who belongs to a *Land* government is determined by the *Land* constitution. Usually, a *Land* government consists of the head of government and the ministers. In Bavaria, secretaries of state are also part of the cabinet. The Berlin Senate consists of the governing mayor and a maximum of eight senators (Art. 55 (2) of the Constitution of Berlin). The government in Baden-Württemberg comprises considerably more persons. In detail, these are the ministers, the secretaries of state, the head of the *Land* chancellery, and the *Land's* representative to the federal government. This currently adds up to 23 persons (as of December 2019).

In principle, anyone who has the right to stand for election can hold a government office (Leunig 2012, p. 159). This means that he or she must not have been sentenced to more than one year's imprisonment in the last five years, he or she must not have been deprived of the right to vote, he or she must not be under legal supervision and must be at least 18 years old. In addition, minimum age limits apply in some *Länder*. In Baden-Württemberg, for example, only those who have reached the age of 35 can be elected minister-president (Art. 46 (1) of the Constitution of Baden-Württemberg), in Bavaria it is even 40 (Art. 44 of the Bavarian Constitution). In addition, there are incompatibilities (Leunig 2012, p. 159), which in Bremen and Hamburg mean that members of the Senate may not simultaneously be members of the *Bürgerschaft* (Art. 108 the Constitution of Bremen; Art. 39 of the Constitution of Hamburg). Their mandates are suspended as long as they belong to the cabinet. But otherwise heads of government and members of government in all *Länder* can belong to the respective parliament. Leunig assumes that simultaneous membership in parliament and government is intended for two reasons. On the one hand, it corresponds to the functional logic of parliamentary systems of government and supports the connection between the government and the government majority; on the other hand, it serves to secure and guarantee the independence of members of government (Leunig 2012, p. 159 f.). Overall, the empirical findings only partially support these assumptions. For example, in NRW between 1947 and 2017 about three out of four members of the government also belonged to the *Land* parliament; in Saarland, however, the proportion has always been well below 60% since the fourth legislative period (1961/65) (Reutter, 2013, p. 55; Rütters, 2012, p. 485).

Apart from the Senate in Bremen, *Land* governments function according to three principles: the minister president principle (which also applies to the Senates in Hamburg and Berlin), the cabinet principle and the departmental principle (*Ministerpräsidenten-, Kabinetts- und Ressortprinzip*). In all *Länder* except Bremen, the head of government has a prominent position (only in Bremen he/she is merely first among equals). He or she has parliamentary legitimation, has—except in Bremen—the authority to issue guidelines, and can appoint and dismiss ministers. For illustration, the case of Brandenburg serves as an example (Anter & Frick, 2016, pp. 106–109). The minister president's pivotal position in the government of Brandenburg is adequately expressed in the Rules of Procedure. According to these Rules and in conjunction with the constitution, the minister-president of this *Land* determines the "guidelines of governmental policy". He or she directs the "business of the *Land* government", must be informed "in good time and on an ongoing basis" of all relevant measures, determines the areas of responsibility of the ministries, appoints and dismisses ministers and, in the event of a tie in the cabinet, has the casting vote. The list could easily be extended. In addition to these legal instruments, prime ministers also have various means of political power: they have public prestige as "Landesvater" or "Landesmutter" ("Father" or "Mother" of a *Land*), usually lead the *Land* party and represent the *Land* externally. To support them, all the heads of government of the *Länder* have set up a so-called "Chancellery", which is called the "Senate Chancellery" in the city states and the "Ministry of State" in Baden-Württemberg. Only the Bavarian Constitution (Art. 52) mentions such a body. But it is everywhere, as Anter and Frick (2016, p. 108) rightly emphasize for Brandenburg: the "center of power". It is the institution where the streams of information converge, it prepares the cabinet meetings and coordinates and directs the work of government. This already points out that in the *Länder*, governing is to be understood above all as a task of coordination and communication.

Minister presidents who were once mocked as "wrens" by Konrad Adenauer (CDU), the first chancellor of the Federal Republic of Germany (Anter & Frick, 2016, p. 105), are nevertheless not able to simply "rule through". On the one hand, only four heads of government have the right to determine the areas of responsibility of ministers or senators. In other cases, the distribution of responsibilities of the *Land* government is decided by the cabinet (Leunig, 2012, p. 160 f.). At the same time, in most *Länder* the parliaments must give their approval to the appointment of either individual members of government or the entire *Land* government. On the other hand, heads of government may have to take coalition agreements into account, as well as claims for representation by regions and party groups. For example, Erwin Teufel (CDU), a popular minister president in Baden-Württemberg at the time, had to go through a second round of voting in his 1996 election, completely unexpectedly, because he had "apparently disappointed some CDU members of parliament" when he wanted to have his cabinet confirmed by the *Landtag* (Obrecht & Haas, 2012, p. 89).

It goes without saying that heads of government do not fulfil the task of guiding and steering alone. For in addition to the prime minister principle, there are the cabinet and the departmental principle (*Kabinettsprinzip* and *Ressortprinzip*) governing the work of *Land* governments. The first states that a *Land* government is a collegial body and can only act jointly. The constitution of Lower Saxony lists a whole range of areas in which the *Land* government decides in this manner (Art. 37 (2) of the Constitution of Lower Saxony). According to this provision, legislative projects are decided by the cabinet by majority vote, as are the delimitation of areas of responsibility and all other tasks legally assigned to the *Land* government (including the appointment of members to the *Bundesrat*). Every head of government, and every minister, requires a majority in the cabinet for his or her policy. At the same time, the ministers manage their departments independently. They have personnel, budgetary and organizational sovereignty and are entitled—within the framework of the guidelines—to shape their policy area autonomously.

6.3.2 Tasks: Steering and Directing

For Wilhelm Hennis (1968, p. 118), the *Länder* were nothing more than "autonomous administrative provinces", because they would exclusively or at least predominantly only implement the laws of the Federation. In this perspective, *Land* governments were nothing more than "administrative executors" (Hennis, 1968, p. 118 f.) or "lord mayorships" (*Oberbürgermeistereien*) (Eschenburg, 1964, p. 226). Klaus-Eckart Gebauer (2006) sees this differently some four decades later. According to Gebauer, *Land* governments are fulfilling their comprehensive mandate to shape the future, both at the *Land*, federal, and European level. They regularly take part in conferences of ministers or prime ministers, exercise important functions in their parties, participate in the *Bundesrat* or are "sought-after discussion partners" (Gebauer, 2006, p. 131). The number of policy areas in which *Land* governments direct and lead is also quite considerable: Hildebrandt and Wolf (2016b) alone list 15 policy areas that are shaped at the *Land* level. They range from school policy to agricultural and transport policy to European and integration policy. The success of *Land* governments in these fields depends on many factors: the government format (one-party or coalition government), the majority in parliament (minority vs. majority government), the coalition agreement, the policies of the federal government, developments in the European Union and other unforeseeable events. The *Land* governments act in three roles (Leunig, 2017; Leunig, 2012, pp. 166–168; Gebauer, 2006): as shapers of policies, as executors of laws, and as heads of *Land* administrations. In addition, there is the representation of the

Land externally (federal government, Europe, abroad), which is discussed below (Sect. 7.2).

Policymaking: Each *Land* government has been given a democratic mandate to shape society in a goal-oriented manner. In election campaigns, the parties compete with their different programs, which they try to translate into effective policies when they are in office. They are therefore not only "executive" or "executing" power, as it is stated in some *Land* constitutions (e.g. Art. 28 (1) of the Constitution of Lower Saxony; Art. 59 (1) of the Constitution of Saxony), but also "shaping power". This is not only a result of their democratic mandate, but they also have the appropriate instruments at their disposal. For they can introduce bills into *Land* parliaments, draft governmental programs, and draw up the budgets of the *Länder*. With these instruments they can react to problems and try to shape society. Since *Land* governments can usually rely on a majority in parliament, the programs and measures adopted in a cabinet can usually be implemented. It becomes particularly difficult when there is a minority government. Under such a constellation, a government is either tolerated by one party (i.e. this party supports the government in individual legislative projects without being represented in the government by ministers) or the government must seek separate support for individual measures (e.g. Leunig, 2017).

However, there are three limitations for *Land* governments. First, the *Länder* are embedded in the federal state structure described in Chap. 2. This means that they can only fulfil their mandate to shape the *Land* in areas defined by constitutional law. In other, important policy areas, the federal government has legislative and formative powers (such as in social policy). Second, the *Länder* have hardly any sources of income of their own and can only dispose to a small extent of the funds allocated to them by the federal government, or within the framework of the federal fiscal equalization system. Most expenditures are predetermined by law. Estimates suggest that just between 5 and 15% of the funds available in a given financial year are at the free disposal of the parliament and the government (Reutter, 2008, p. 290). Third, *Land* governments must take coalition agreements and internal party majorities into account. This requires intensive and often small-scale coalition and conflict management, which takes place in the cabinets, through the chancelleries and in so-called "coalition committees". Some also see the latter as the actual "power center" of a coalition government (Leunig, 2017, p. 127).

Implementation of laws: As mentioned above, *Land* governments must implement laws passed by parliament. As a rule, this does not lead to any potential for conflict, since in parliamentary systems of government a majority of deputies support the government, which in any case brings most of the laws into the *Land* parliaments. This can become problematic in the case of a minority government (Leunig, 2017) or if the parliamentary majority has a different political orientation than the government. Such a constellation occurred in Hesse in 2008/2009. The *Land* government, led at the time by Roland Koch (CDU), lost its majority in the *Land* elections on January 7, 2008. Since the red-green minority government planned by Andrea Ypsilanti (SPD), which should have been tolerated by the PDS, did not receive a majority in Parliament (4 SPD members of parliament refused to vote for Ypsilanti), Roland Koch and his *Land* government remained in office. Thus, a parliamentary majority consisting of SPD, Greens and Left Party stood against the *Land* government led by the CDU. This could not go well. In November 2008, the Hessian Landtag was therefore dissolved, and new elections were held on January 18, 2009.

Head of administration: Finally, *Land* governments are the head of *Land* administrations (Leunig, 2017, p. 129; Jesse et al., 2014, pp. 187–208). *Land* administrations implement federal and *Land* laws (in part this task is also assigned to local self-government; Holtmann et al., 2017). The *Länder* thus execute three types of laws:

- *Land laws* are implemented under its own direction and according to rules it has issued itself. Only the general legal framework (such as basic rights, principles of the rule of law, etc.) applies here.
- *Länder* can execute *federal laws* in their own right (Art. 84 of the Basic Law): With such laws the federation issues a regulation (e.g. on social welfare), which the *Länder* then have to implement administratively. If necessary, they can delegate this to the local self-administration or have it carried out by authorities of the state. In any case, the *Länder* regulate the "establishment of authorities and the administrative procedure" (Article 84 (2) of the Basic Law) in these laws on their own authority. The federal government may only exercise legal supervision here (Article 84 (3) of the Basic Law).
- Finally, *Länder* can execute federal laws on federal commission (Article 85 of the Basic Law): Such laws are implemented by the *Land* on behalf of the Federation (e.g. generation and use of nuclear energy under Article 87c of the Basic Law). Here, the establishment of the necessary authorities remains a matter for the *Länder*, although the federal government may issue administrative regulations. Moreover, federal supervision extends not only to the legality but also to the expediency of implementation.

Against this background, it is hardly surprising that in 2018, around 50% of those employed in the public sector were working in the *Länder* and only around 10% were employed by the federal government (the remainder worked in local government [31%] or in social insurance agencies [9%]) (https://www.bmi.bund.de/DE/themen/oeffentlicher-dienst/zahlen-daten-fakten/zahlen-daten-fakten-node.html).

The *Land* administrations are structured differently. Generalizations are difficult, if only because of the differences in size between *Länder*. The city-states differ from the area states and the large area states from the small ones. In the city-states of Berlin, Hamburg and Bremen, *Land* governments and district administrations perform administrative tasks. In the large *Flächenländer* (area states), three levels can be distinguished that belong to the *Land* administration (Bogumil & Jann, 2009, p. 100f.; Jesse et al., 2014, p. 187–208). At the top are the so-called supreme *Land* authorities and higher *Land* authorities. In Saxony, the former include the *Land* government, the prime minister and the ministries which set up the *Land* authorities (Article 83 of the Constitution of Saxony) and "direct" and "supervise" them (Jesse et al., 2014, p. 199). The latter include, for example, the *Land* Statistical Office, the *Land* Office for the Protection of the Constitution, or the *Land* Office of Criminal Investigation. Below this administrative top level there are the so-called general *Land* central authorities. In Saxony, this level is called *Landesdirektion (Land* Administration). In other *Länder* these are known as regional councils or district governments. This middle level also includes specialized authorities such as the *Oberfinanzdirektion* ("Regional Financial Directorate"). These authorities are directly subordinate to the ministries and have coordination and control functions (Bogumil & Jann, 2009, p. 100). This middle administrative level still existed in seven large territorial *Länder* in 2009 (Bogumil & Jann, 2009, p. 101). At the lowest level there are special administrations such as finance or forestry offices, as well as authorities of the general *Land* administration like district offices and district administrations. Smaller *Flächenländer* such as Saarland do not have central authorities.

6.4   *Land* Constitutional Courts: The Judicial Power

The Federation has five supreme courts, two federal courts and the Federal Constitutional Court (Articles 94–96 of the Basic Law). All the other of the total of 1,086 courts that existed in the Federal Republic of Germany in 2018 are established and maintained by the *Länder*. All *Land* constitutions contain provisions on the administration of the judicial system, the election and appointment of judges, the prosecution of judges and constitutional courts. This federal structure of the rule of law has many consequences. Apparently, courts' judgements differ from region to region (Grundies, 2018). However, this dimension of judicial power cannot be addressed in this context. The further description is limited to the highest courts in the *Länder*: the constitutional courts. All *Länder* have a constitutional court (Table 6.2), which in eight *Länder* is called the *Land* Constitutional Court (*Landesverfassungsgericht),* in three *Länder* the State Court (*Staatsgerichtshof),* and in five *Länder* the Constitutional High Court (*Verfassungsgerichtshof).* (The former State Court of Baden-Württemberg was renamed and became the Constitutional High Court in 2015). Like *Land* parliaments and *Land* governments, they are constitutional bodies. Their composition, their competences and their establishment are regulated in the respective *Land* constitution. All *Länder* have also passed corresponding implementing laws with provisions: on the term of office of judges, on election procedures, on the composition and qualifications of judges, on the position and organization of the court, and on its competences. And all *Land* constitutional courts have also adopted rules of procedure to regulate internal procedures (such as how to proceed when judges are absent).

Land constitutional courts have a mandate and duty to interpret the basic legal orders of the *Länder* in a binding manner and to examine whether state action

Table 6.2 *Land* constitutional courts: constitutional foundations, size and resources (as of May 2016). (*Source* Reutter, 2020a, p. 160)

	Constitution	Seat	Article in constitution	Number of justices	Staff[a]	Budget[a]
BW	1955	Stuttgart	68	9	2	378,000
BAV[b]	1947	Munich	60–69	38	(3)	n.a
BER	1992	Berlin	84	9	6	695,700
BB	1993	Potsdam	112–114	9	6	843,700
BRE	1949	Bremen	139–140	7	0	46,000
HAM	1953	Hamburg	65	9	[c]0	52,000
HES	1948	Wiesbaden	130–133	11	2	691,600
MW	1995	Greifswald	52–54	7	1	196,400
LS	1957	Bückeburg	54–55	9	n.a	202,000
NRW	1952	Münster	75–76	7	n.a	58,000
RP[b]	1947	Koblenz	130–136	9	n.a	n.a
SLD	1959	Saarbrücken	96–97	8	0	24,500
SAY	1993	Leipzig	81	9	0	193,600
SAT	1993	Dessau-Roßlau	74–76	7	n.a	354,200
SH	2008	Schleswig	51	7	0	47,000
TH	1995	Weimar	79–80	9	4	389,600

[a]Non-judicial staff (civil servants, employees and manual workers) or appropriations entered in the budget for 2016 excluding judges
[b]In Bavaria and Rhineland-Palatinate, the constitutional courts are budgeted in the budget of the Ministry of Justice as part of the administrative jurisdiction or at the Munich Higher Regional Court
[c]The dual budget of the Hanseatic City does not include any posts, but the homepage of the State Court lists three academic staff members

complies with the constitution.[4] Like the Federal Constitutional Court, the *Land* constitutional courts thus decide on disputes "in which political law is disputed and the political itself becomes the subject of judicial assessment on the basis of existing norms" (Statusbericht, 1957, p. 145). This fundamental characterization of the *Land* constitutional jurisdiction is undisputed. It is, however, unclear whether and how effectively *Land* constitutional courts fulfill the mission outlined above. Whether they are thus able to effectively enforce the constitution. This question will be pursued in two steps: First, the election procedures and composition of the judiciary as well as the functioning of the *Land* constitutional courts are examined (Sect. 6.4.1). Finally, the areas of competence are outlined (Sect. 6.4.2.).

---

[4]The rest is based on Reutter (2017b) and (2018a); see also Reutter (2020c) and Dombert (2012).

6.4.1   Structure and Mode of Operation

In Rhineland-Palatinate and Bremen, the president of the respective Higher Administrative Court is simultaneously a member of the constitutional courts of these two *Länder* (Glaab, 2017, p. 275; Ketelhut, 2017). Otherwise, since 2017 the judges of all constitutional courts must be legitimized in democratic election procedures. Since the parliaments in the *Länder* are the only institutions elected by the sovereign, such legitimation can only take place there. However, parliamentary elections raise a problem. Judges are supposed to be independent. Judgments may be passed in the "name of the people", but not on their behalf, and certainly not in the name or on behalf of the parliament.

The *Länder* have—not surprisingly—regulated the election, composition, and term of office of constitutional judges differently. The main motives behind these regulations were: to guarantee the qualification of the judges, to prevent the court from being instrumentalized by political parties and to secure its democratic legitimacy. Irrespective of the common motives that apply in all *Länder*, considerable differences can be found at all stages of the electoral process: Even the criteria for eligibility show differences (Table 6.3). Four *Länder* have a minimum age of 40 years, eleven of 35. Ten *Länder* have a maximum age of 65, 68, or 70. The right to nominate judges for election to parliament varies as well: this can be done by the *Land* government, parliamentary groups, committees, individual members of parliament, the presidium or council of elders, or the courts. Finally, in seven *Land* parliaments a majority of two thirds of the legal members is required for the election of constitutional judges; in four a majority of two thirds of the votes cast, in three a majority of the legal members, in one a relative majority (most votes) and in three a simple majority of the votes cast. Except in Hesse, judges are elected by the plenum of the *Land* parliament. It always takes place without debate and by secret ballot. As analyses show, the elections of the judges are usually, but by no means always, without problems. Every now and then individual candidates fail or need a second ballot. Sometimes elections are also held late (Weigl, 2017, pp. 60 f.; Reutter, 2017c, pp. 81–83).

The eligibility requirements mentioned above are complemented by provisions on the composition of constitutional courts. In principle, it should be noted that constitutional judges in all *Länder* work on an honorary basis. They are not employed by the courts and at best receive an expense allowance for their office. In their main profession they are judge at a specialized court, university professor of law at a university (or college of higher education), lawyer, or they exercise another non-legal profession. The budgets are correspondingly small, fluctuating between 24,500 and 800,000 Euros for the year 2016.

Ignoring Bavaria, the courts consist of 7 to 11 judges. In most constitutional courts lay judges can also participate.[5] At the same time, most *Länder* provide

---

[5]According to § 5 of the German Judges Act, the qualification for the office of judge is awarded to those who have completed the second state examination in law.

Table 6.3 Eligibility, number, composition and terms of office of constitutional judges in the *Länder*. (*Source* Reutter, 2020b, pp. 206 and 220)

	Minimum age	Maximum age[a]	Eligibility Parliament	Number of professional judges	Number of lay judges[b]	Gender quota[c]	Term of office[d]	Re-election
BW	–	–/–		3	3	0	9	Yes
BAV[b]	40	–/(65)	Landtag	23	0	0	8/LP	Yes
BER	35	–/–	Bundestag	3	(3)	3	7	No
BB	35	68/68	Bundestag	3	(3)	(3)	10	No
BRE	35	–/(65)	Bundestag	3	(4)	0	LP	Yes
HAM	40	–/(65)	Bürgerschaft	4	(3)	0	6	Yes
HES	35	–/(65)	Landtag	5	(6)	0	7/LP	Yes
MW	35	68/68	Landtag	2	(3)	0	12	No
LS	35	–/–	Landtag	3	(3)	(3)	7	Yes
NRW	35	–/65	Landtag	3	0	0	10	No
RP[b]	35	70/65	Landtag	4	(5)	0	6	Yes
SLD	35	–/–	Landtag	2	0	(3)	6	Yes
SAY	35	70/65	Bundestag	5	(4)	0	9	Yes
SAT	40	–/–	Landtag	3	(4)	(3)	7	Yes
SH	40	–/–	Bundestag	3	0	0	6	Yes
TH	35	68/68	Landtag	3	(3)	0	7	Yes

[a]Maximum age for non-judicial members/maximum age for professional judges

[b]In () the number of judges who may or may not be qualified to hold judicial office, i.e. who may or may not be lay judges

[c]Number of judges who must be female, in () number of judges who should be female

[d]Years/legislative period (= LP)

for a minimum number of professional judges. Professional judges are full-time judges at a specialized court and part-time judges at the constitutional court. This is intended to combine constitutional and specialized jurisdiction and to guarantee the highest possible quality of constitutional case-law. In five *Länder*, a gender quota is also provided for at least as a "target provision". Finally, in Brandenburg, an "adequate representation of proposals from the political forces of the *Land* shall be striven for in the election" of constitutional judges (Art. 112 (4) of the Constitution of Brandenburg); in Bremen and Berlin, the parliamentary groups have the right to propose candidates for elections of constitutional judges. In the *Länder*, the statutory term of office of constitutional judges is between 6 and 12 years; in Bremen, Bavaria and Hesse, at least some of the justices must be newly elected at the beginning of each legislative period (Weigl, 2017, pp. 59 f.; Koch-Baumgarten, 2017, pp. 183–185; Ketelhut, 2017, pp. 137 f.). Re-election is ruled out in four *Länder*, in five *Länder* a one-time re-election is possible, and in seven *Länder* constitutional justices may be re-elected as often as desired. The average justice is male, well over 50 years of age and is qualified to hold the office of judge.

Constitutional courts deal with political disputes and their justices are elected by political institutions in political procedures. However, their functioning and status are decidedly apolitical. For they are not only constitutional, that is, political bodies, but also courts and thus institutions free of politics. They are to make their decisions solely in accordance with the law and are fundamentally independent. However, only a few *Land* constitutional courts can dispose of their own organizational structure; most of them are affiliated to other specialized courts whose services and personnel they use.

Decisions are generally made in plenary, i.e. in the assembly of all judges (the only exception is the Bavarian Constitutional Court with its three chambers structured according to competencies). Most decisions are taken by resolution without a hearing. Some *Land* constitutional courts also have a chamber that can dismiss inadmissible or obviously unfounded constitutional complaints.

6.4.2   Tasks: Constitution and Politics

Everybody knows Karlsruhe as the seat of the Federal Constitutional Court, and every person even moderately interested in politics has seen on television how eight judges dressed in red robes enter a courtroom paneled with wood and announce their decision on highly political matters. But who even knows the seat of the *Land* constitutional courts, let alone their decisions? Nevertheless, *Land* constitutional courts also have influence on politics, on parliament and government. This influence varies according to political realms and *Land* (Reutter, 2020c). Even the different case numbers hardly allow for generalizations. For example, the Constitutional High Court in Bavaria has made around nine times as many decisions as its counterpart in Rhineland-Palatinate. And the Constitutional Court in Bremen takes on average about one decision per year, in Berlin it is over

170 (Weigl, 2017, p. 67; Ketelhut, 2017; Glaab, 2017; Reutter, 2017c, p. 94). Differences between the constitutional courts can be worked out on the basis of the types of proceedings (a) and the roles (b) that constitutional courts can assume (for further details, see Reutter, 2018a).

(a) Abstract and concrete judicial review, disputes between high state organs, review of election results, and conflicts over direct-democratic procedures are the most important types of procedures, and thus the core area of constitutional jurisdiction in the *Länder*. The individual constitutional complaint, which is also known by the Federal Constitutional Court and which can be lodged by "anyone" who feels that his or her fundamental rights have been violated, can be lodged in 11 *Länder* and local constitutional complaints in 13 *Länder*. Other competences (such as ministerial impeachments, impeachments of members of parliament, review of the admissibility of constitutional amendments, etc.) are assigned to only a few constitutional courts and have so far remained practically irrelevant.

(b) If one examines the consequences of constitutional court decisions on *Land* policy, three roles can be distinguished. They can become "arbitrators" when they resolve disputes between high state organs (Flick, 2011; Carstensen, 2020). They act as "negative legislators" (Kelsen, 2008) when they declare a law passed by the *Land* parliament to be unconstitutional. In these cases, a constitutional court becomes active in shaping the law, but in a negative form. Important decisions have repeatedly been brought about in the course of such proceedings. Finally, constitutional courts are most important institutions in the judicial system; citizens can turn to them with a constitutional complaint if they feel their fundamental rights have been violated. Only a few constitutional complaints are honored with success.

It is true that other types of procedures, such as the review of election results, can also radiate into the political arena (Blumenthal, 2017; Plöhn, 2020). But the cursory overview shows that *Land* constitutional courts do not qualify as substitute legislators. In the *Länder*, policy-making is the task of the executive and legislative branches.

The *Länder,* the Federation, and Europe

7

Abstract

The *Länder* are members of a supreme state that is itself a member of the European Union. Such a constellation does not make democratic governance any easier. It again points to the tension between diversity and unity inherent in the federal state. This chapter asks how unity in German federalism can be established under the conditions of European integration. The presentation is limited to the participation of the *Länder* in the *Bundesrat* (Federal Council) and to other types of policy coordination between the *Länder,* and between the *Länder* and the federal government. Finally, the role of the *Länder* in the European Union is outlined.

7.1   The *Bundesrat:* The Chamber of the *Länder* within the Federation

The *Bundesrat* is an unusual institution. In international comparison, it is even unique (Sturm, 2012). The Federal Council is a "perpetual" constitutional body. Its composition changes with each new Land government and it knows neither legislative periods nor definable intervals between meetings. The *Bundesrat* met for the first time on September 7, 1949. Some 70 years later, on September 20, 2019, the 980th session of this constitutional body took place. On average, this was just under 14 meetings per year. So, the Bundesrat meets in plenary session every three to four weeks, with up to 80 items on the agenda. This is a tight schedule that cannot be managed without preparation, prearranged consultation, and a high degree of discipline in the sessions. This already addresses central aspects of the *Bundesrat:* its composition (a), its working methods (b) and its competences (c).

(a) In the *Bundesrat,* the *Länder* are represented by their *Land* governments (Grasl, 2016; Leunig & Träger, 2012; Schmidt, 2012). By international standards,

© Springer Fachmedien Wiesbaden GmbH, part of Springer Nature 2021
W. Reutter, *The German Länder*, https://doi.org/10.1007/978-3-658-33681-3_7

it is quite unusual for a body that plays a crucial role in legislation to consist of representatives of the executive branch. Members of *Land* governments can belong to the *Bundesrat* (Sect. 3.3). In most cases, these are the minister-presidents and the ministers (in the city states, they are the mayors and the senators). In the Bavarian Constitution, however, the Land government also includes secretaries of state (Article 43 (2)), who can then also belong to the *Bundesrat.* The *Land* governments nominate the members or their deputies for the *Bundesrat.*

The members of the *Bundesrat* are not parliamentarians. They receive—as members of the *Bundesrat*—no parliamentary allowance,[1] enjoy neither immunity nor indemnity. This is also logical. For the *Bundesrat* is not a parliament and the members of the *Bundesrat* are, so to speak, envoys of their government. They are bound by the decisions of their *Land* governments. The imperative mandate applies. In the Parliamentary Council this kind of representation was chosen for historical reasons and because it seemed to make sense that the *Länder,* which execute most of the laws, should be involved in the legislation. The interests of the *Länder* and their experience in implementing laws were to be incorporated into federal legislative procedures at an early stage. At the same time, it was guaranteed that the concerns of the federal government would also be taken into account in the *Länder* (Krumm, 2015, p. 173; Laufer & Münch, 2010, pp. 137–141).

In the Parliamentary Council, there was controversy over the distribution of votes in the *Bundesrat* from the beginning. Some argued that each *Land* should have the same number of votes in the *Bundesrat* (like the states in the American Senate). Then little Bremen would have had as many votes as big North Rhine-Westphalia. Here, the *Länder* would have been considered solely as units under state law. The other option was to calculate the votes in the *Bundesrat* on the basis of the number of inhabitants, i.e. to take account of the principle of representativeness. This would now have meant that the populous *Länder* would have been able to dominate the *Bundesrat.* This option did not find a majority either. Finally, the so-called "weakened Bundesrat solution" (*abgeschwächte Bundesratslösung*), which consisted of taking into account the number of inhabitants only in a modified, weakened form, was capable of compromise. This regulation is still in force, although it was slightly modified in the course of German unification. According to the current version, each *Land* has at least three votes, regardless of the number of inhabitants. Depending on the number of inhabitants, the number of votes increases to four, five or a maximum of six (the latter if a Land has at least seven million inhabitants). This immediately raises the question of whether the *Länder* are adequately represented under such a construction (Krumm, 2015, pp. 173–175; Sturm, 2001, pp. 53–69).

At the beginning of 2020, the *Bundesrat* had 69 members (Table 7.1), with the approximately 0.8% of Germany's inhabitants who live in Bremen represented by three members in the *Bundesrat.* This accounts for 4.3% of the votes

---

[1]They are allowed to use public transport free of charge, receive reimbursement of travel costs and a fairly modest flat-rate allowance; see: Laufer and Münch (2010, p. 139).

Table 7.1 Bundesrat: votes and population shares (as of 2018). (*Source* Statistisches Bundesamt, 2019b; www.bundesrat.de; own calculations and additions)

	Current government (as of 01/2020)[a]	Number of votes in the *Bundesrat*	Population 2018 (in thousands)	Percentage of total population	Share of votes in the *Bundesrat*	Inhabitants per vote
BW	Greens/CDU	6	11,070	13.3	8.7	1,845,000
BAV	CSU/FW	6	13,077	15.8	8.7	2,179,500
BER	SPD/Left/ Greens	4	3,645	4.4	5.8	911,250
BB	SPD/CDU/ Greens	4	2,512	3.0	5.8	628,000
BRE	SPD/Greens/ Left	3	683	0.8	4.3	227,667
HAM	SPD/Greens	3	1,841	2.2	4.3	613,667
HES	CDU/Greens	5	6,266	7.5	7.2	1,253,200
MW	SPD/CDU	3	1,610	1.9	4.3	536,667
LS	SPD/CDU	6	7,982	9.6	8.7	1,330,333
NRW	CDU/FDP	6	17,933	21.6	8.7	2,988,833
RP	SPD/FDP/ Greens	4	4,085	4.9	5.8	1,021,250
SLD	CDU/SPD	3	991	1.2	4.3	330,333
SAY	CDU/Greens/ SPD	4	4,078	4.9	5.8	1,019,500
SAT	CDU/SPD/ Greens	4	2,208	2.7	5.8	552,000
SH	CDU/Greens/ FDP	4	2,897	3.5	5.8	724,250
TH[b]	Left/SPD/ Greens	4	2,143	2.6	5.8	535,750
Total	–	69	83,021	100.0	100.0	1,203,203

[a]FW = Freie Wähler (Party of Free Voters)
[b]The government was in office on a managing basis in January 2020; since February 5, 2020, Thomas Kemmerich (FDP) alone has represented the *Land* in the *Bundesrat;* he did not attend the 985th session of the *Bundesrat* on February 14, 2020

of the *Bundesrat*. North Rhine-Westphalia, the most populous state in the Federal Republic with almost 18 million inhabitants, has six votes in the Bundesrat. This means that around one fifth of Germany's inhabitants account for 8.7% of the votes in the *Bundesrat*. Small states are therefore over-represented in the *Bundesrat*, large ones under-represented.

In the *Bundesrat*, *Land* governments are supposed to represent interests of the *Länder*. However, *Land* governments inevitably consist of party politicians. And it is quite possible that the interests of a *Land* may be different from the interests of a government. Gerhard Lehmbruch's thesis discussed in Chap. 3 is based on this possible divergence between party politics and *Land* interests in the *Bundesrat,* and this concept shaped research on the *Bundesrat* (and the federal state) in Germany. We will come back to this again.

(b) Working methods: The functioning of the *Bundesrat* is shaped by its composition and the associated voting rules. One should not forget the committees in which the bills are discussed and in which—in contrast to the plenary session of the *Bundesrat*—specialist officials can also sit who are appointed by the *Land* governments. The plenary debates are characterized by this just as much as the committee discussions. Confrontational arguments are the exception and frowned upon. A factual, problem-oriented style of debate dominates. A distinctive feature of *Bundesrat* meetings is the calm tone in which debates take place. The atmosphere is subdued rather than heated; people talk calmly. Heckling is rare, and so far, the president did not have to request order at any time (or only in very exceptional circumstances). Expressions of displeasure or applause, which until the beginning of the 1990s were almost considered contrary to the house style, are hardly to be heard even in more recent times. In such terms the Bundesrat describes itself quite accurately (https:// www.bundesrat.de/DE/bundesrat/br-plenum/br-plenum-node.html).

Voting in the Bundesrat is based on two principles. On the one hand, the members of the Bundesrat vote as the the *Land* governments have determined in advance. Thus, the vote is fixed before the representatives of the Land governments meet in the Bundesrat. This can pose problems if the *Land* government consists of a coalition that cannot agree on a unified position. In such cases, coalition agreements usually contain a so-called *Bundesrat* clause, according to which the *Land* must abstain in the *Bundesrat* if the coalition partners fail to come to an agreement (Sturm, 2001, pp. 54–55). However, an abstention works like a no-vote in *Bundesrat* votes. This is because a majority of the statutory members of the *Bundesrat* is required to pass a resolution. On the other hand and linked to this is the uniform casting of votes (Article 51 of the Basic Law), which is done by proxy. This means that it is sufficient if the votes of a *Land* are cast by a representative of this *Land*. Votes of a *Land* cannot be split, but always only be cast as a block. The potential for conflict is increased in the case of so-called "mixed coalitions", i.e. *Land* governments consisting of parties that are in opposition and in government at the federal level (e.g. the coalition of the Greens and the CDU in Baden-Württemberg, which has existed since 2016, the former being in opposition at the federal level and the latter being in government).

(c) The role of the *Bundesrat* in legislation is controversial. The *Bundesrat* can either wield a suspensive or an absolute veto the laws passed by the *Bundestag.* The first can therefore come into being without the *Bundesrat* having cast a positive vote on them (or having voted on them at all). With laws requiring consent this is not possible. Here the *Bundesrat* must give its approval with the majority of its votes. This is why the *Bundesrat* is referred to as a "blocking instrument" or "veto player" or as the cause for gridlock and the venue in which the structural conflicts between party competition and the federal state materializes (Lehmbruch, 2000; Burkhart, 2008). These are far-reaching conclusions, supported above all by the fact that the proportion of laws requiring approval is considered by many to be far too high and to exceed by far the extent that the fathers and mothers of the Basic Law would have imagined. Leaving aside the fact that it is not entirely clear what the fathers and mothers of the Basic Law really envisaged and whether their ideas were particularly realistic, it is important against this background to take a closer look at the role of the *Bundesrat* and thus of the *Länder* in the Federation. Five aspects are important here:

Firstly, the procedure in the *Bundesrat* is fundamentally based on consensus. Thus, the *Bundesrat* can intervene in the legislative process at an early stage. All bills which the Federal Government introduces into the *Bundestag* must be submitted in advance to the *Bundesrat* for its opinion. The *Bundesrat* can then comment on the draft within six weeks (Article 76 (2) of the Basic Law). (This period can be shortened to three weeks; in the case of bills amending the Basic Law it is nine weeks). The *Bundestag* or the federal government are thus aware of possible concerns of the *Länder* at an early stage.

Secondly, the *Bundesrat* may "three weeks after receipt of the legislative resolution request that a committee composed of members of the Bundestag and the Bundesrat be convened for the joint consideration of bills" (Article 77 (2) of the Basic Law). This is the so-called mediation committee. It was once quite strikingly called the "dark room" of the legislative procedure (Reutter, 2006b, p. 13), because it negotiates in camera. It is composed of 16 members of the *Bundesrat* and the same number of members of the *Bundestag*. This mediation committee tries to find a compromise and, if necessary, to bring about an amendment to the legislative resolution. And the committee is amazingly successful. Of the 322 bills discussed in this committee between 1994 and 2017, 280 could be promulgated. That was over 86% (own calculations according to: Bundesrat, 2017).

Thirdly, in the relevant literature, the power of the *Bundesrat* in legislative procedures is inferred solely from the nature of the law and from the fact that, in the case of laws requiring consent, the chamber of the *Länder* has vetoed them or could have done so. In this perspective, the laws that the *Bundesrat* can only wield with a suspensive veto are usually neglected or considered unimportant. According to the Basic Law (Article 77 (3)), these laws do not require approval because they do not affect vital interests of the *Länder*. This used to be about 40% of all laws; currently it is more than 60% of all laws passed by the *Bundestag*. A suspensive veto requires the majority of the votes of the *Bundesrat* (Article 52 (3) of the Basic Law). However, this is considered a less promising instrument. For objections can be rejected by the *Bundestag* with the same majority with which the *Bundesrat* has lodged its objection. Consequently, the *Bundesrat* could also block legislative decisions of the *Bundestag* in the case of opposition bills. For this it would have to object with a two-thirds or even larger majority. Objections with such a majority are practically non-existent. Thus, between 1994 and 2017, just 44 objections were raised, of which 40 were rejected by the *Bundestag* (out of a total of 1706 objection bills before the *Bundesrat;* Bundesrat, 2017). Whatever the reasons, the result—few objections and even fewer laws that failed because of an objection—puts into perspective the generalized assessment that the *Bundesrat* is an instrument of obstruction.

Fourthly, a similar conclusion is reached when analysing the laws that require approval. These are laws, the *Bundesrat* can wield with an absolute veto. So, unlike objection laws, the *Bundesrat* must pass a resolution on such laws. Here, too, a majority of the members of the *Bundesrat* is required. This is where the party political constellation comes into play. For it is indeed the exception that the party-political majorities in the *Bundestag* and *Bundesrat* coincide. For example, although the grand coalition of CDU/CSU and SPD in the *Bundestag* had a comfortable majority of over 56% of all MPs in January 2020, there were only three *Länder* (MW, LS, SLD) at that time in which a grand coalition of CDU and SPD also governed. These three *Länder* together had elelven votes in the *Bundesrat*. In contrast, in January 2020, the Greens, who were in opposition in the *Bundestag*, were in a coalition government in eleven *Länder*. These eleven *Länder* had 45 votes. In short, without the support of the Greens, no law requiring approval could be passed in the *Bundesrat* in early 2020. And such a constellation is by no means the exception. *Divided government*, i.e. different party-political majorities in the *Bundesrat* and *Bundestag,* is the rule. Against this background, it can only come as a surprise that only a few laws passed by the *Bundestag*—around 2%—fail due to a lack of approval by the *Bundesrat*.[2]

Fifthly, for the sake of completeness, it should finally be mentioned that the *Bundesrat* itself can introduce bills into the *Bundestag*. And this it does. In total, between 1994 and 2017 (13th–18th term of the *Bundestag*), the Bundesrat forwarded 599 bills to the *Bundestag* for resolution via the federal government. Only about one in five of the bills introduced by the *Bundesrat* was adopted by the *Bundestag* and made into law by the Federal President (Bundesrat, 2017; Münch, 2011). As mentioned, the *Bundesrat* also participates in the administration of the Federation (Article 51 (1) of the Basic Law). Here, too, it can withhold its consent to statutory ordinances or administrative regulations, although this almost never happens. Of 2881 statutory ordinances and 261 administrative regulations that were forwarded to and deliberated by the *Bundesrat* between 1994 and 2017, only 17 statutory ordinances and 4 administrative regulations failed due to a lack of consent by the *Bundesrat*.

7.2   Horizontal and Vertical Coordination: The *Länder* in the Federation and in Europe

As mentioned at the beginning, in the federal state not only the diversity of the constituent *Länder* is to be preserved, but also the unity of the state as a whole is to be guaranteed. This unification takes place in various forms and, of course, also through mechanisms that are not part of the federal one, such as the social security

---

[2]According to the *Bundesrat*, between 1994 and 2017 (13th to 18th legislative periods of the *Bundestag*), a total of 1483 laws requiring consent were passed; the *Bundesrat* refused consent for 90 bills; 28 laws passed by the *Bundestag* were not promulgated (Bundesrat, 2017).

	Vertical (including federal government)	Horizontal (without federal government)
Formal / institutionalized	(1) Federal Council, joint tasks, on federal commission, etc.	(2) "Third level"; Conference of minister presidents, Conference of Ministers of Education and Cultural Affairs, treaties between Länder, administrative agreements
Informal	(3) Länder representations, professional fraternities across levels; departmental cronies	(4) Ministerial conferences, working groups and advisory bodies

Fig. 7.1 Political and administrative interdependence in Germany: levels and forms. (*Source* after Bogumil & Jann, 2009, p. 83)

system, the jurisdiction of the Federal Constitutional Court or other federal policy measures. But the *Länder* also play an active role in the formation of unity. The federal government and *Land* governments are intertwined in different ways and in varying compositions (Fig. 7.1). The relevant literature distinguishes between the forms (informal/formal) and levels (horizontal/vertical) of cooperation.

(1) We have already dealt with some of these interdependencies, such as the *Bundesrat* and the commissioned administration. These two forms are institutionalized and include both levels of government (i.e. federal and *Land* government). Another manifestation is the so-called joint tasks *(Gemeinschaftsaufgaben)*, which were incorporated into the Basic Law in 1969 and which Fritz W. Scharpf and others (1976) regarded as the prime example of policy interdependence (Sect. 3.3). Joint tasks are characterized by the fact that they are of importance to the "whole" and that the "participation of the Federation is necessary for the improvement of living conditions" (Article 91a (1) of the Basic Law). Although the tasks of improving the regional economic structure, the agricultural structure and coastal protection fundamentally remain tasks of the *Länder,* the federal government has an impact here through partial funding and through framework planning (Bogumil & Jann, 2009, p. 81). Laufer and Münch (2010, p. 192) rightly describe joint tasks as the "most intensive form of cooperation in the German federal state".

(2) A further formal—albeit horizontal—coordination exists in the Minister Presidents' Conference (MPC), in which, of course, the mayors of the city states also participate. The conference was convened for the first time after the founding of the Federal Republic at the end of 1952 (corresponding meetings also took place before 1949). As a rule, the heads of government of all 16 Länder meet four times a year. Twice a year the Federal Chancellor is invited to a meeting following the MPC.[3] These conferences are prepared by the state or senate chancelleries of the *Länder*. The chairmanship of the MPC rotates annually in a fixed order, with

---

[3]The information comes from: https://www.bayern.de/staatsregierung/ministerpraesidentenkonferenz/die-ministerpraesidentenkonferenz/.

Krumm (2015, p. 184) reporting that between 10 and 15 agenda items are dealt with per meeting. If necessary, *Land* treaties or federal—*Land* agreements can be prepared and decided within this framework. This so-called "third-level cooperation" is a double-edged undertaking (Laufer & Münch, 2010, pp. 184 f.; Sturm, 2001, pp. 78–80; Kropp, 2010, pp. 134–153). Behind this cooperation is the problem that many societal challenges cannot be tackled within the borders of a *Land*. Cooperation across *Land* borders is therefore imperative. At the same time, this form of cooperation calls into question the claim for autonomy of the *Länder* and promotes unitarization tendencies.

Before the Federal Republic of Germany, there were not only the *Länder* but also the Standing Conference of the Ministers of Education and Cultural Affairs. The "Standing Conference of the Ministers of Education and Cultural Affairs of the Länder in the Federal Republic of Germany" was founded in 1948 by the ministers of education and cultural affairs of the *Länder* in the western occupation zone (Laufer & Münch, 2010, p. 186). It attempts—with little success—in particular to coordinate the school and higher education policies of the *Länder* and is based on voluntarism and unanimity. These design principles give each *Land* the possibility to prevent resolutions. This institution was maintained after the founding of the Federal Republic of Germany and became a model for many other conferences of ministers, which take place annually (or more often, if necessary). The Federal Government participates here as a guest if necessary.

(3 and 4) In addition to these formal interlinking structures, there are informal ways of coordination. In addition to the Minister Presidents' Conferences, there are various conferences of specialist ministers which also take place at regular intervals. Unlike the Standing Conference of the Ministers of Education and Cultural Affairs of the *Länder*, these conferences do not have an organizational substructure. Decisions of these bodies are not binding. According to Laufer and Münch (2010, p. 184) the sole purpose of these bodies is to discuss problems together, to make positions clear and thus also to contribute to mutual understanding. Representatives of the *Länder* to the federal level and other network-like structures (professional fraternities and departmental cronies) complete these informal types of cooperation.

European integration poses a particular challenge for the *Länder*. According to Roland Sturm and Heinrich Pehle (2012, p. 98), German federalism is in danger of becoming a "folkloristic remnant" due to European integration. This is because *Länder* would increasingly lose independent "room for maneuver" and scope for shaping policy (ibid.). According to Martin Große-Hüttmann (2019, pp. 141–143), however, the *Länder* were quite capable of developing European political agency and increasing their influence in this field. According to Große-Hüttmann, the *Länder* successfully defended their rights and competences with a "leave-us-alone strategy". They insisted on their legislative competences, emphasized the principle of subsidiarity, or participated in EU policy in the Committee on European Union Questions of the Bundesrat. At the same time, the *Länder* succeeded with a "let-us-in strategy" in securing rights of representation in European decision-making

	EU level	National level
"Leave-us-alone"-strategy	Subsidiarity principle (including early warning system); clear delimitation of competences	Land participation via Art. 23 of the Basic Law; horizontal coordination via conferences of the prime ministers and specialist ministers
"Let-us-in"-strategy	Land observers, "sideline foreign policy", lobbying at EU level, information offices in Brussels, Committee of the Regions; networking of regions with legislative powers	Participation of the Länder via Article 23 of the Basic Law; vertical coordination between the Federation and Länder

Fig. 7.2 European policy strategies and options for action of the *Länder.* (*Source* Große-Hüttmann, 2019, p. 141.)

procedures (Article 23 (6) of the Basic Law) and in the European Committee of the Regions. In some cases, they have even pursued a kind of "sideline foreign policy" and built up an independent network of contacts and information independent of the federal government (Sturm & Pehle, 2012, pp. 103–114; Große-Hüttmann, 2019; Hrbek, 2017; Fig. 7.2).

The *Länder*, Democracy, and Federalism in Germany

8

Abstract

Finally, the contribution of the *Länder* to democracy and federalism is summarized. I will bring to the fore whether, and to what extent, *Länder* provide opportunities for democratic participation, contribute to the integration of society, and have an impact on the separation of powers.

In his seminal work on Germany's political system, Manfred G. Schmidt (2011, pp. 467–498) analyzed the "achievements and shortcomings of politics in Germany". According to Schmidt (2011, p. 498), the Federal Republic of Germany thereby earns "overall good marks for its political institutions in general". Although Schmidt also discusses the federal state in this context, he only deals with the *Länder* in passing. Nevertheless, following Schmidt, it can be summed up: The *Länder*, too, have contributed to the Germany's postwar "success story" (Sontheimer et al., 2007, pp. 413–423). They are "pillars of democracy" in the Federal Republic of Germany. They not only founded democracy in 1949, but they also steadily contribute to its stability and efficiency (and sometimes also cause problems). Constitutionally, the contribution of the *Länder* to democracy is already expressed in the fact that German federalism must be democratic and is endowed with a guarantee of eternity. The participation of the *Länder* in the functioning of the democratic federal state is noticeable in several ways (for the following see: Reutter, 2008, pp. 341–344): Firstly, in an international comparison, the Federal Republic of Germany can be described as participation-friendly (Schmidt, 2011, pp. 478–472). In this context, participation means the chance for the sovereign to actively take part in public decision-making at the federal level as well as in the *Länder* (and in the EU). In this respect, it supports the integration of society as a whole.

© Springer Fachmedien Wiesbaden GmbH, part of Springer Nature 2021
W. Reutter, *The German Länder*, https://doi.org/10.1007/978-3-658-33681-3_8

This classification can be justified not only by the still high turnout in elections to the Bundestag, but also by elections to *Land* parliaments (as well as local parliaments) and direct democratic procedures. The "people" can therefore participate democratically at different levels and in varying forms. That is no small achievement. However, this is also accompanied by a potential for endangering democracy when parties like the AfD that reject fundamental values of the federal constitution succeed in *Länder*.

Secondly, (regional) social interests and concerns can be represented and moderated via *Land* parties and *Land* parliaments. This results in a kind of "division of labor" between the federal and Land levels. Regional conflicts can be dealt with regionally, and regionally limited problems can be solved with regionally limited means and measures. This relieves the burden on federal policy.

Thirdly, it should be mentioned that most parties govern and oppose a government at the same time. That is, they can be involved in government at the federal level or in one *Land* and at the same time be in opposition in another *Land*. This means that parties fit into the democratic order of rule in different roles (unless they fundamentally reject this order). This, too, can promote overall social integration.

Fourthly, democracy means rule for a limited period of time. Changes of government and power are therefore an imperative part of it and they should be "orderly, procedurally accurate and without bloodshed" (Schmidt, 2011, p. 473). After 1949, the *Länder* have helped to make such changes to a political standard practice (Decker & Blumenthal, 2002, pp. 162–164). They happen frequently and—mostly—as just described.

Finally, there is the innovation function and the contribution of the *Land* parliaments to administrative control. Innovations by the *Länder* include constitutional regulations or political constellations (new coalitions and coalition formats). But also in some policy fields, *Länder* have made a name for themselves as "laboratories". This increases the "learning" and "error-correcting" capacity in German democracy, an element that is even reflected in policy fields that are highly centralized (Schmidt, 2011, pp. 490–492). Diversity in the German federal state can thus not only be the cause of conflicts and tensions, but also the basis for solutions and problem solving.

Annotated Literature

Freitag, M., & Vatter, A. (eds.) (2008). *Die Demokratien der deutschen Bundesländer. Politische Institutionen im Vergleich.* **Barbara Budrich.**

This volume examines the political systems in the Länder based on the distinction between consensus and majoritarian democracy, which is familiar from international comparative research. This results in theoretically and empirically comprehensive and substantial inventories of the "patterns of democracy" in German federalism.

"Gleichwertige Lebensverhältnisse". *Aus Politik und Zeitgeschichte,* **Vol. 69. No. 46, November 11, 2019.**

In six contributions, this issue introduces a central guiding idea of German federalism: the demand for "equality of living conditions". It deals with theoretical questions about this guiding concept, methodological problems in measuring living conditions and discusses political consequences of this constitutional mandate.

Hartmann, J. (ed.). Handbuch der deutschen Bundesländer. (3rd ed.). Campus 1997.

The handbook edited by Jürgen Hartmann provides basic information on all 16 Länder. The contributions on the Länder follow a uniform scheme and deal with constitutional foundations, socio-economic developments, and political structures. In addition, selected policy areas are presented. The volume contains a chapter on German federalism.

Hildebrandt, A., & Wolf, F. (Eds) (2016). *Die Politik der Bundesländer. Zwischen Föderalismusreform und Schuldenbremse* **(2nd ed.). Springer VS.**

The first edition of this anthology still had the subtitle: "State Activity in Comparison". The change in the subtitle refers to a change in perspective. While the first edition was intended to elaborate and explain the differences between the

© Springer Fachmedien Wiesbaden GmbH, part of Springer Nature 2021
W. Reutter, *The German Länder,* https://doi.org/10.1007/978-3-658-33681-3

Länder in policy fields and political structures, the new edition published in 2016 focuses on the "central question" of whether and how the federalism reforms of 2006 and 2009 have left an impact in the Länder. In addition to the introduction and final chapter, a total of 17 contributions provide a comprehensive insight into the policy fields covered.

Laufer, H., & Münch, U. (2010). *Das föderale System der Bundesrepublik Deutschland*. Bayerische Landeszentrale für politische Bildungsarbeit.

This problem-oriented introduction illuminates and explains all crucial aspects of German federalism. In addition to the historical development, the structural and functional principles of federalism (distribution of tasks, political interdependence, Bundesrat), the book also deals with the German Länder in the European Union and the financial order in the German federal state.

Leunig, S. (2012). *Die Regierungssysteme der deutschen Länder im Vergleich* (2nd ed.). Springer VS.

In his textbook, Leunig provides a comparative overview of the governmental systems in the countries. Leunig presents the origins of the countries and focuses on the institutional design of the political orders. In particular, Leunig points out that the systems of government differ between the countries, even though they have typological similarities.

Pestalozza, C. (ed.) (2014). *Verfassungen der deutschen Bundesländer mit dem Grundgesetz* (10th ed. as of 1 March 2014). C.H. Beck.

The volume contains an introductory contribution by the editor, the text editions of all 16 state constitutions as well as the Basic Law.

Reutter, W., (2008). *Föderalismus, Parlamentarismus und Demokratie. Landesparlamente im Bundesstaat.* Barbara Budrich.

This volume examines the consequences of the democratic and unitary federal state for the state parliaments. In detail, it describes the emergence and role of state constitutions, the electoral and party systems, questions of parliamentary sociology, the structure, functioning and function of the state parliaments, as well as how these institutions fit into the German and European multi-level system.

***Reutter, W.* (2017). Landesverfassungsgerichte. Entwicklung—Aufbau— Funktionen. Springer VS.**

In addition to the introduction, the volume contains contributions on all 16 state constitutional courts. The contributions examine the origins, structure and tasks of these supreme courts in the states.

References

Abromeit, H. (1992). *Der verkappte Einheitsstaat*. Westdeutscher Verlag.

Algasinger, K., Oertzen, J.v., & Schöne, H. (2004). Wie das Parlament die Regierung kontrolliert: Der Sächsische Landtag als Beispiel. In E. Holtmann & W. J. Patzelt (Eds.), *Kampf der Gewalten? Parlamentarische Regierungskontrolle—gouvernmentale Parlamentskontrolle. Theorie und Empirie* (pp. 106–147). VS Verlag.

Anderson, G., & Scheller, H. (2012). *Fiskalföderalismus. Eine international vergleichende Einführung*. Budrich (UTB).

Anter, A., & Frick, V. (2016). Die Landesregierung in Brandenburg. In A. Lorenz, A. Anter & W. Reutter, *Politik und Regieren in Brandenburg* (pp. 105–122). Springer VS.

Arbeitskreis „Volkswirtschaftliche Gesamtrechnungen der Länder" (2019). *Gesamtwirtschaftliche Ergebnisse im Bundesländervergleich*. Statistisches Landesamt Baden-Württemberg. https://vgrdl.de/VGRdL/tbls/VGR_FB.pdf. Accessed 4 Dec 2019.

Arnim, H.H.v. (2002). *Vom schönen Schein der Demokratie. Politik ohne Verantwortung—am Volk vorbei*. Droemer Knaur.

Austermann, D. (2019). Schafft die Länder ab, denn so war der Föderalismus nicht gedacht! Ein Plädoyer zur Änderung des Grundgesetzes. *Zeitschrift für Parlamentsfragen, 50*(2), 434–437. https://doi.org/10.5771/0340-1758-2019-2-434.

Bagehot, W. (1993). *The English Constitution [1867]. With an Introduction by Richard Crossman*. Fontana Press.

Behnke, N. (2015). Stand und Perspektiven der Föderalismusforschung. *Aus Politik Und Zeitgeschichte, 28–30*, 9–16.

Behnke, N., & Kropp, S. (Eds.) (2016). *Ten years of federalism reform in Germany*. Special Issue of *Regional and Federal Studies, 26*(5).

Benz, A. (2009). Ein gordischer Knoten der Politikwissenschaft? Zur Vereinbarkeit von Föderalismus und Demokratie. *Politische Vierteljahresschrift, 50*(1), 3–22.

Benz, A., & Kropp, S. (2014). Föderalismus in Demokratien und Autokratien—Vereinbarkeiten, Spannungsfelder und Dynamiken. *Zeitschrift für Vergleichende Politikwissenschaft, 8*(1), 1–27.

Benz, W. (1989). *Von der Besatzungsherrschaft zur Bundesrepublik. Stationen einer Staatsgründung 1946–1949*. Fischer.

Benz, W. (1994). *Potsdam 1945. Besatzungsherrschaft und Neuaufbau im Vier-Zonen-Deutschland* (3rd ed.). dtv.

Bertelsmann-Stiftung (2008). *Bürger und Föderalismus. Eine Umfrage zur Rolle der Bundesländer*. Verantwortlich: O. Wintermann & T. Petersen. Bertelsmann-Stiftung. https://www.bertelsmann-stiftung.de/fileadmin/files/BSt/Presse/imported/downloads/xcms_bst_dms_23798_23799_2.pdf. Accessed 2 Sept 2019.

Bertelsmann-Stiftung (Ed.) (2015a). *Prekäre Wahlen—Bremen. Milieus und soziale Selektivität der Wahlbeteiligung bei der Bremischen Bürgerschaftswahl 2015*. Bertelsmann-Stiftung.

https://www.bertelsmann-stiftung.de/fileadmin/files/BSt/Publikationen/GrauePublikationen/ Studie_ZD_Prekaere-Wahlen-Bremen_2015.pdf. Accessed 13 Dec 2019.

Bertelsmann-Stiftung. (2015b). *Prekäre Wahlen—Hamburg. Milieus und soziale Selektivität der Wahlbeteiligung bei der Hamburger Bürgerschaftswahl 2015.* Bertelsmann-Stiftung. https:// www.bertelsmann-stiftung.de/de/publikationen/publikation/did/prekaere-wahlen-hamburg/. Accessed 13 Dec 2019.

Bertelsmann-Stiftung (2017). *Populäre Wahlen—NRW. Mobilisierung und Gegenmobilisierung der sozialen Milieus bei der Landtagswahl Nordrhein-Westfalen 2017.* Bertelsmann-Stiftung. https://www.bertelsmann-stiftung.de/fileadmin/files/BSt/Publikationen/GrauePublikationen/ ZD_Populaere_Wahlen_NRW.pdf. Accessed 13 Dec 2019.

Beyme, K.v. (1997a). Funktionswandel der Parteien in der Entwicklung von der Massenmitgliederpartei zur Partei der Berufspolitiker. In O. W. Gabriel, O. Niedermayer & R. Stöss (Eds.), *Parteiendemokratie in Deutschland* (pp. 359–383). Bundeszentrale für politische Bildung.

Beyme, K.v. (1997b). *Der Gesetzgeber. Der Bundestag als Entscheidungszentrum.* Westdeutscher Verlag.

Beyme, K. v. (1999). *Die parlamentarische Demokratie. Entstehung und Funktionsweise 1789–1999* (3rd ed.). Westdeutscher Verlag.

Blumenthal, J.v. (2009). *Das Kopftuch in der Landesgesetzgebung. Governance im Bundesstaat zwischen Unitarisierung und Föderalisierung.* Nomos.

Blumenthal, J.v. (2017). Das Hamburgische Verfassungsgericht. In W. Reutter (Ed.), *Landesverfassungsgerichte. Entwicklung—Aufbau—Funktionen* (pp. 149–174). Springer VS.

BMI (ed.) (2019). *Unser Plan für Deutschland - Gleichwertige Lebensverhältnisse überall - Schlussfolgerungen von Bundesminister Horst Seehofer als Vorsitzendem sowie Bundesministerin Julia Klöckner und Bundesministerin Dr. Franziska Giffey als Co-Vorsitzenden zur Arbeit der Kommission „Gleichwertige Lebensverhältnisse".* Stand: Juli 2019. https://www.bmi.bund.de. Accessed 2 Dec 2019.

Böckenförde, E.-W. (1992). *Staat, Verfassung, Demokratie. Studien zur Verfassungstheorie und zum Verfassungsrecht.* Suhrkamp.

Bödeker, S. (2012). *Soziale Ungleichheit und politische Partizipation in Deutschland. Grenzen politischer Gleichheit in der Bürgergesellschaft.* Arbeitspapier Nr. 1. Otto-Brenner-Stiftung. http://www.otto-brenner-stiftung.de. Accessed 10 March 2013.

Bogumil, J., & Jann, W. (2009). *Verwaltung und Verwaltungswissenschaft in Deutschland. Einführung in die Verwaltungswissenschaft* (2nd ed.). Springer VS.

Braun, D. (2004). Föderalismus. In L. Helms & U. Jun (Eds.), *Politische Theorie und Regierungslehre. Eine Einführung in die politikwissenschaftliche Institutionenforschung* (pp. 130–162). Campus.

Bundesrat. (2017). Die Arbeit des Bundesrates im Spiegel der Zahlen. (Stand 22. November 2017). https://www.bundesrat.de/DE/dokumente/statistik/statistik-node.html. Accessed 13 Jan 2020.

Burkhart, S. (2008). *Blockierte Politik. Ursachen und Folgen von „Divided Government" in Deutschland.* Campus

Burkhart, S., & Manow, P. (2006). *Was bringt die Föderalismusreform? Wahrscheinliche Effekte der geänderten Zustimmungspflicht.* MPIFG Working Paper 06/6. Max-Planck-Institut für Gesellschaftsorschung. https://www.mpifg.de/pu/workpap/wp06-6/wp06-6.html. Accessed 6 Oct 2006.

Carstensen, C. (2020). Parlamentsrechtliche Entscheidungen von Landesverfassungsgerichten in Organstreitverfahren. In W. Reutter (Ed.). *Verfassungsgerichtsbarkeit in Bundesländern. Theoretische Perspektiven, methodische Überlegungen und empirische Befunde* (pp. 237–262). Springer VS.

Carstensen, F., & Schüttemeyer, S. S. (2015). Reden und Handeln! Zur Zukunft des Landesparlamentarismus. In Thüringer Landtag (Ed.), *Ein Vierteljahrhundert parlamentarische Demokratie. Der Thüringer Landtag 1990–2014* (pp. 282–314). Wartburg Verlag.

Decker, F. (2010). Parteien im politischen System der Bundesrepublik Deutschland. In A. Kost, W. Rellecke & R. Weber (Eds.), *Parteien in den deutschen Ländern* (pp. 71–99). Beck.

Decker, F., & Blumenthal, J.v. (2002). Die bundespolitische Durchdringung von Landtagswahlen. Eine empirische Analyse von 1970 bis 2001. *Zeitschrift für Parlamentsfragen, 33*(1), 144–165.

Detterbeck, K. (2019). Parteienwettbewerb und Bundesstaatlichkeit. Die Strukturbruch-These und der Wandel des deutschen Parteiensystems. In Europäisches Zentrum für Föderalismus-Forschung Tübingen (Ed.), *Jahrbuch des Föderalismus 2019. Föderalismus, Subsidiarität und Regionen in Europa* (pp. 101–112). Nomos.

Detterbeck, K., & Renzsch, W. (2008). Symmetrien und Asymmetrien im bundesdeutschen Parteienwettbewerb. In U. Jun, M. Haas & O. Niedermayer (Eds.), *Parteien und Parteiensysteme in den deutschen Ländern* (pp. 39–56). VS Verlag.

Dombert, M. (2012). Landesverfassungen und Landesverfassungsgerichte in ihrer Bedeutung für den Föderalismus. In I. Härtel (Ed.), *Handbuch Föderalismus—Föderalismus als demokratische Rechtsordnung und Rechtskultur in Deutschland, Europa und der Welt* (pp. 19–38). Springer.

Duverger, M. (1959). *Die politischen Parteien*. Mohr Siebeck.

Eder, C., & Magin, R. (2008). Direkte Demokratie. In M. Freitag & A. Vatter (Eds.), *Die Demokratien der deutschen Bundesländer* (pp. 257–308). Budrich.

Eicher, H. (1988). *Der Machtverlust der Landesparlamente. Historischer Rückblick, Bestandsaufnahme, Reformansätze*. Duncker & Humblot.

Eilfort, M. (2006). Landes-Parteien: Anders, nicht verschieden. In H. Schneider & H.-G. Wehling (Eds.), *Landespolitik in Deutschland. Grundlagen—Strukturen—Arbeitsfelder* (pp. 207–224). VS für Sozialwissenschaften.

Elster, J. (1994). Die Schaffung von Verfassungen: Analyse der allgemeinen Grundlagen. In U.K. Preuß (Ed.), *Zum Begriff der Verfassung. Die Ordnung des Politischen* (pp. 37–57). Fischer.

Esche, F., & Hartmann, J. (Eds.) (1997). *Handbuch der deutschen Bundesländer* (3rd ed.). Campus.

Eschenburg, T. (1964). Parlamentarische Regierung in den Ländern. In T. Eschenburg (Ed.), *Zur politischen Praxis in der Bundesrepublik. Kritische Betrachtungen 1957 bis 1961* (pp. 223–227). Piper.

Faus, R., Mannewitz, T., Storks, S., Unzicker, K., & Vollmann, E. (2019). *Schwindendes Vertrauen in Politik und Parteien. Eine Gefahr für den gesellschaftlichen Zusammenhalt?* Bertelsmann-Stiftung. https://www.gesellschaftlicher-zusammenhalt.de. Accessed 4 Dec 2019.

Feldkamp, M. F. (Ed.). (1999). *Die Entstehung des Grundgesetzes für die Bundesrepublik Deutschland 1949. Eine Dokumentation*. Philipp Reclam jun.

Flick, M. (2008). Landesverfassungen und ihre Veränderbarkeit. In M. Freitag & A. Vatter (Eds.), *Die Demokratien der deutschen Bundesländer. Politische Institutionen im Vergleich* (pp. 221–236). Budrich.

Flick, M. (2011). *Organstreitverfahren vor den Landesverfassungsgerichten. Eine politikwissenschaftliche Untersuchung*. Lang.

Fraenkel, E. (1991). *Deutschland und die westlichen Demokratien*. Edited by A. v. Brünneck. Suhrkamp.

Freitag, M., & Vatter, A. (2008). Die Bundesländer zwischen Konsensus- und Mehrheitsdemokratie: Eine Verortung entlang ihrer politisch-institutionellen Konfigurationen. In M. Freitag & A. Vatter (Eds.), *Die Demokratien der deutschen Bundesländer. Politische Institutionen im Vergleich* (pp. 309–328). Budrich.

Gebauer, K.-E. (2006). Landesregierungen. In H. Schneider & H.-G. Wehling (Eds.), *Landespolitik in Deutschland. Grundlagen—Strukturen—Arbeitsfelder* (pp. 130–147). VS für Sozialwissenschaften.

Glaab, M. (2013). Direkte Demokratie in Bayern—Traditionslinien und aktuelle Tendenzen. In M. Glaab & M. Weigl (Eds.), *Politik und Regieren in Bayern* (pp. 251–256). Springer VS.

Glaab, M. (2017). Der Verfassungsgerichtshof Rheinland-Pfalz. In W. Reutter (Ed.), *Landesverfassungsgerichte. Entwicklung—Aufbau—Funktionen* (pp. 269–296). Springer VS.

Glaab, M., & Weigl, M. (Eds.) (2013). *Politik und Regieren in Bayern.* Springer VS.

Glaeßner, G.-J. (2006). *Politik in Deutschland.* (2nd ed.). VS Verlag..

Grasl, M. (2016). Neue Möglichkeiten: Die Bundes- und Europapolitik der Länder. In A. Hildebrandt & F. Wolf (Eds.), *Die Politik der Bundesländer. Zwischen Föderalismusreform und Schuldenbremse* (2nd ed.; pp. 161–181). Springer VS.

Grimm, D. (1994). *Die Zukunft der Verfassung* (2nd ed.). Suhrkamp.

Große-Hüttmann, M. (2019). Als Bundesstaat im EU-Mehrebenensystem: die „Koevolution" von Europäischer Union und deutschen Föderalismus seit 1949. In Europäisches Zentrum für Föderalismus-Forschung Tübingen (Ed.), *Jahrbuch des Föderalismus 2019. Föderalismus, Subsidiarität und Regionen in Europa* (pp. 127–144). Nomos.

Grube, N. (2009). Nähe und Distanz: Föderale Einstellungen der Bevölkerung in 60 Jahren Bundesrepublik Deutschland. In Europäisches Zentrum für Föderalismus-Forschung Tübingen (Ed.), *Jahrbuch des Föderalismus 2009. Föderalismus, Subsidiarität und Regionen in Europa* (pp. 149–160). Nomos.

Grundies, V. (2018). Regionale Unterschiede in der gerichtlichen Sanktionspraxis in der Bundesrepublik Deutschland. Eine empirische Analyse. In D. Hermann & A. Pöge (Eds.), *Kriminalsoziologie. Handbuch für Wissenschaft und Praxis* (pp. 295–316). Nomos. https://doi.org/10.5771/9783845271842-458.

Haas, M., Jun, U., & Niedermayer, O. (2008). Die Parteien und Parteiensysteme der Bundesländer. In U. Jun, M. Haas, & O. Niedermayer (Eds.), *Parteien und Parteiensysteme in den deutschen Ländern* (pp. 9–38). VS Verlag.

Habermas, J. (1991). *Erläuterungen zur Diskurstheorie.* Suhrkamp.

Habermas, J. (1993). *Strukturwandel der Öffentlichkeit. Untersuchungen zu einer Kategorie der bürgerlichen Gesellschaft* (3rd ed.). Suhrkamp.

Härtel, I. (2012). Die Gesetzgebungskompetenzen des Bundes und der Länder im Lichte des wohlgeordneten Rechts. Grundlagen des Föderalismus und der deutsche Bundesstaat. In I. Härtel (Ed.), *Handbuch Föderalismus—Föderalismus als demokratische Rechtsordnung und Rechtskultur in Deutschland, Europa und der Welt* (pp. 527–610). Springer.

Helms, L. (1995). Parteiensysteme als Systemstruktur. Zur methodisch-analytischen Konzeption der funktional-vergleichenden Parteiensystemanalyse. *Zeitschrift für Parlamentsfragen, 26*(4), 642–657.

Helms, L. (2007a). Gerhard Lehmbruch, Parteienwettbewerb im Bundesstaat. Regelsysteme und Spannungslagen im Institutionengefüge der Bundesrepublik. In S. Kailitz (Ed.), *Schlüsselwerke der Politikwissenschaft* (pp. 233–236). VS Verlag.

Helms, L. (2007b). *Die Institutionalisierung der liberalen Demokratie.* Campus.

Helms, L., Eppler, A., & Willumsen, D. M. (2017). Is there a „German school" of comparative politics. An institutional perspective. *Zeitschrift für Vergleichende Politikwissenschaft, 11*(4), 533–556. https://doi.org/10.1007/s12286-017-0349-6. Accessed 15 Nov 2019.

Hennis, W. (1968). Parlamentarische Opposition und Industriegesellschaft. Zur Lage des parlamentarischen Regierungssystems. In W. Hennis, *Politik als praktische Wissenschaft. Aufsätze zur politischen Theorie und Regierungslehre* (pp. 105–125). Piper.

Herzog, R. (1997). *Aufbruch ins 21. Jahrhundert. Berliner Rede 1997 von Bundespräsident Roman Herzog.* Hotel Adlon, Berlin, 26. April 1997. https://www.bundespraesident.de/SharedDocs/Reden/DE/Roman-Herzog/Reden/1997/04/19970426_Rede.html. Accessed 19 Dec 2019.

Hesse, K. (1962). *Der unitarische Bundesstaat.* C.F. Müller.

Hesse, K. (1993). *Grundzüge des Verfassungsrechts der Bundesrepublik Deutschland.* (19th ed.). C.F. Müller.

Hesse, J. J., & Ellwein, T. (2012). *Das Regierungssystem der Bundesrepublik Deutschland.* (10th ed.). Nomos.

Heußner, H.K., & Jung, O. (Eds.) (1999). *Mehr direkte Demokratie wagen. Volksbegehren und Volksentscheid. Geschichte—Praxis—Vorschläge*. Olzog.

Hildebrandt, A. (2016). Die Finanzpolitik der Länder nach den Föderalismusreformen: Begrenzte Spielräume, fortdauernde Unterschiede. In A. Hildebrandt & F. Wolf (Eds.), *Die Politik der Bundesländer. Zwischen Föderalismusreform und Schuldenbremse* (2nd ed., pp. 115–138). Springer VS.

Hildebrandt, A., & Wolf, F. (2006a). Die Potenziale des Bundesländervergleichs. In A. Hildebrandt & F. Wolf (Eds.), *Die Politik der Bundesländer. Staatstätigkeit im Vergleich* (pp. 11–20). VS Verlag.

Hildebrandt, A., & Wolf, F. (Eds.). (2006b). *Die Politik der Bundesländer. Staatstätigkeit im Vergleich*. VS Verlag.

Hildebrandt, A., & Wolf, F. (2016a). Die Politik in den Bundesländern unter reformierten institutionellen Rahmenbedingungen. In A. Hildebrandt & F. Wolf (Eds.), *Die Politik der Bundesländer. Zwischen Föderalismusreform und Schuldenbremse* (2nd ed., pp. 11–20). Springer VS.

Hildebrandt, A., & Wolf, F. (Eds.). (2016b). *Die Politik der Bundesländer. Zwischen Föderalismusreform und Schuldenbremse* (2nd ed.). Springer VS.

Hölscheidt, S. (1995). Die Praxis der Verfassungsverabschiedung und der Verfassungsänderung in der Bundesrepublik. *Zeitschrift für Parlamentsfragen, 26*(1), 58–84.

Holtmann, E. (2007). Dehnungen der Gewaltenteilung im modernen Verfassungsstaat. Zum Gestaltwandel der Gewaltenteilung aus theoretischer und empirischer Sicht. In S. Kropp & H.-J. Lauth (Eds.), *Gewaltenteilung und Demokratie* (pp. 110–120). Nomos.

Holtmann, E., & Patzelt, W. J. (Eds.). (2004). *Kampf der Gewalten. Parlamentarische Regierungskontrolle—gouvernementale Parlamentskontrolle. Theorie und Empirie*. VS Verlag.

Holtmann, E., Rademacher, C., & Reiser, M. (2017). *Kommunalpolitik. Eine Einführung*. Springer VS.

Hough, D., & Jeffery, C. (2003). Landtagswahlen: Protestwahlen oder Regionalwahlen. *Zeitschrift für Parlamentsfragen, 34*(1), 79–94.

Hrbek, R. (2017). Die Rolle der Länder und des Bundesrates in der deutschen Europapolitik. In K. Böttger & M. Jopp (Eds.), *Handbuch zur deutschen Europapolitik* (pp. 131–148). Bundeszentrale für politische Bildung.

Hrbek, R. (2019). Die Konstituierung der Bundesrepublik Deutschland als Bundesstaat: Bestimmungsfaktoren und Entscheidungen 1945-1949. In Europäisches Zentrum für Föderalismus-Forschung Tübingen (Ed.), *Jahrbuch des Föderalismus 2019. Föderalismus, Subsidiarität und Regionen in Europa* (pp. 39–52). Nomos.

Isensee, J. (1991). Abstimmen, ohne zu entscheiden? Ein Plebiszit über die Verfassung ist nicht vorgesehen und auch nicht wünschenswert. In B. Guggenberger & T. Stein (Eds.), *Die Verfassungsdiskussion im Jahr der deutschen Einheit. Analysen, Hintergründe, Materialien* (pp. 214–219). Hanser.

Jellinek, G. (1914). *Allgemeine Staatslehre (=Recht des modernen Staates* (vol. 1, 3rd ed.). Digitalisat.

Jesse, E., Schubert, T., & Thieme, T. (2014). *Politik in Sachsen*. Springer VS.

Jun, U. (1993). Landesparlamente. In J. Bellers & R. Graf von Westphalen (Eds.), *Parlamentslehre. Das parlamentarische Regierungssystem im technischen Zeitalter* (pp. 489–513). R. Oldenbourg.

Jun, U. (1994). *Koalitionsbildung in den deutschen Bundesländern. Theoretische Betrachtungen, Dokumentation und Analyse der Koalitionsbildungen auf Länderebene seit 1949*. Leske + Budrich.

Jun, U. (2013). Typen und Funktionen von Parteien. In O. Niedermayer (Ed.), *Handbuch Parteienforschung* (pp. 119–114). Springer VS.

Jun, U., Haas, M., & Niedermayer, O. (Eds.). (2008). *Parteien und Parteiensysteme in den deutschen Ländern*. VS Verlag.

Jung, O. (1994). *Grundgesetz und Volksentscheid*. Westdeutscher Verlag.

Jung, O. (1997). Die Volksabstimmungen über die Länderfusion Berlin-Brandenburg: Was hat sich bewährt—wer ist gescheitert? *Zeitschrift für Parlamentsfragen, 28*(1), 13–20.

Jung, O. (2012). Direkte Demokratie und Föderalismus. Probleme, Reformen, Perspektiven des deutschen Föderalismus. In I. Härtel (Ed.), *Handbuch Föderalismus—Föderalismus als demokratische Rechtsordnung und Rechtskultur in Deutschland, Europa und der Welt* (Vol. II, pp. 223–248). Springer.

Kaiser, A. (2012). Politiktheoretische Zugänge zum Föderalismus. Grundlagen des Föderalismus und der deutsche Bundesstaat. In I. Härtel (Ed.), *Handbuch Föderalismus—Föderalismus als demokratische Rechtsordnung und Rechtskultur in Deutschland, Europa und der Welt* (Vol. I, pp. 165–178). Springer.

Kelsen, H. (2008). *Wer soll Hüter der Verfassung sein* [1930/31]? Edited by Robert Chr. van Ooyen. Mohr Siebeck.

Ketelhut, J. (2017). Verfassungsgerichtsbarkeit im Zwei-Städte-Staat. Der Staatsgerichtshof der Freien Hansestadt Bremen. In W. Reutter (Ed.), *Landesverfassungsgerichte. Entwicklung—Aufbau—Funktionen* (pp. 129–148). Springer VS.

Kirbach, R. (2002). Konsens beim Thema Kormorane. Die Zeit, Nr. 17 vom 18.4.2002. https://zeus.zeit.de/text/archiv/2002/17/200217_landtage.xml. Accessed 12 Jan 2005.

Klatt, H. (2004). Reformbedürftiger Föderalismus in Deutschland? Beteiligungsföderalismus versus Konkurrenzföderalismus. In H.-G. Wehling (Ed.), *Die deutschen Länder. Geschichte, Politik, Wirtschaft* (3rd ed., pp. 9–16). VS Verlag.

Klecha, S. (2010). *Minderheitsregierungen in Deutschland*. Edited by Friedrich-Ebert-Stiftung. Hannover. https://library.fes.de/pdf-files/bueros/hannover/08122.pdf. Accessed 15 May 2013.

Kleßmann, C. (1991). *Die doppelte Staatsgründung. Deutsche Geschichte 1945–1955*. Bundeszentrale für politische Bildung.

Koch-Baumgarten, S. (2017). Der Staatsgerichtshof in Hessen zwischen unitarischem Bundesstaat, Mehrebenensystem und Landespolitik. In W. Reutter (Ed.), *Landesverfassungsgerichte. Entwicklung—Aufbau—Funktionen* (pp. 175–198). Springer VS.

Köcher, R. (2012). Föderalismus im Spiegel der Demoskopie. Entfaltungsbereiche des Föderalismus. In I. Härtel (Ed.), *Handbuch Föderalismus—Föderalismus als demokratische Rechtsordnung und Rechtskultur in Deutschland, Europa und der Welt* (Vol. III, pp. 749–763). Springer-Verlag.

Kocka, J. (1999). Asymmetrical historical comparison: The case of the German Sonderweg. *History and Theory, 38*(1), 40–50.

Köhler, G. (1988). *Historisches Lexikon der deutschen Länder. Die deutschen Territorien vom Mittelalter bis zur Gegenwart*. Beck.

Köhler, H. (2005). *Fernsehansprache von Bundespräsident Horst Köhler am 21. Juli 2005*. https://www.bundespraesident.de/SharedDocs/Reden/DE/Horst-Koehler/Reden/2005/07/20050721_Rede_Anlage2.pdf?__blob=publicationFile&v=2. Accessed 10 Sep 2019.

Korte, K.-R. (2003). *Wahlen in der Bundesrepublik Deutschland* (4th ed.). Bundeszentrale für politische Bildung.

Kost, A. (Ed.). (2005). *Direkte Demokratie in den deutschen Ländern. Eine Einführung*. VS Verlag.

Kost, A., Rellecke, W., & Weber, R. (Eds.). (2010). *Parteien in den Bundesländern. Geschichte und Gegenwart*. Beck.

Kriele, M. (1994). *Einführung in die Staatslehre. Die geschichtlichen Legitimitätsgrundlagen des demokratischen Verfassungsstaates* (5th ed.). Westdeutscher Verlag.

Kropp, S. (1997). Die Länder in der bundesstaatlichen Ordnung. In O.W. Gabriel & E. Holtmann (Eds.), *Handbuch des politischen Systems der Bundesrepublik Deutschland* (pp. 247–288). Oldenbourg.

Kropp, S. (2001). *Regieren in Koalitionen. Handlungsmuster und Entscheidungsbildung in deutschen Länderregierungen*. Westdeutscher Verlag.

Kropp, S. (2010). *Kooperativer Föderalismus und Politikverflechtung.* VS Verlag.

Kropp, S., & Sturm, R. (1998). *Koalitionen und Koalitionsvereinbarungen. Theorie, Analyse und Dokumentation.* Westdeutscher Verlag.

Krumm, T. (2015). *Föderale Staaten im Vergleich. Eine Einführung.* Springer VS.

Laakso, M., & Taagepera, R. (1979). „Effective" number of parties. A measure with application to West Europe. *Comparative Political Studies, 12*(1), 3–27.

Landtag Brandenburg (2010). *Namen—Daten—Fakten. 5. Wahlperiode. 2009–2014.* Landtag Brandenburg.

Laufer, H., & Münch, U. (2010). *Das föderale System der Bundesrepublik Deutschland* (8th ed.). Bayerische Landeszentrale für politische Bildungsarbeit.

Lehmbruch, G. (2000). *Parteienwettbewerb im Bundesstaat. Regelsysteme und Spannungslagen im politischen System der Bundesrepublik Deutschland* (3rd ed.). Westdeutscher Verlag.

Lempp, J. (2010). Berlin—die Parteien im „wiedervereinigten Bundesland". In A. Kost, W. Rellecke & R. Weber (Eds.), *Parteien in den deutschen Ländern. Geschichte und Gegenwart* (pp. 161–173). Beck.

Leonhard, W. (1966). *Die Revolution entläßt ihre Kinder* (8th ed.). Ullstein.

Leunig, S. (2012). *Die Regierungssysteme der deutschen Länder im* Vergleich (2nd ed.). Springer VS.

Leunig, W. (2017). Die Landesregierung von Sachsen-Anhalt: Aufgaben und Strukturen des politischen Machtzentrums. In H. Träger & S. Priebus (Eds.), *Politik und Regieren in Sachsen-Anhalt* (pp. 125–144). Springer VS. https://doi.org/10.1007/978-3-658-13689-5_9.

Leunig, S., & Reutter, W. (2012). Länder und Landesparlamente im föderalen System der Bundesrepublik Deutschland. Grundlagen des Föderalismus und der deutsche Bundesstaat. In I. Härtel (Ed.), *Handbuch Föderalismus—Föderalismus als demokratische Rechtsordnung und Rechtskultur in Deutschland, Europa und der Welt* (Vol. I, pp. 743–766). Springer.

Leunig, S., & Träger, H. (Eds.). (2012). *Parteipolitik und Landesinteressen. Der deutsche Bundesrat 1949–2009.* LIT.

Ley, R. (2010). Die Wahl der Ministerpräsidenten in den Bundesländern. *Zeitschrift für Parlamentsfragen, 41*(2), 390–420.

Ley, R. (2015). Die Wahl von Ministerpräsidenten ohne Landtagsmandat. Fallbeispiele und Überlegungen zur geplanten Verfassungsänderung in NRW. *Zeitschrift für Parlamentsfragen, 46*(1), 100–116.

Ley, R. (2016). Wahl der Ministerpräsidenten von Mecklenburg-Vorpommern, Brandenburg, Sachsen-Anhalt, Sachsen und Thüringen. *Zeitschrift für Parlamentsfrage, 47*(3), 573–606.

Lijphart, A. (1999). *Patterns of Democracy. Government Forms and Performance in Thirty-Six Countries.* Yale University Press.

Lincoln, A. (1994). *Gettysburg address: 19. November 1863. Mit einem Essay von Ekkehart Krippendorff.* Europäische Verlagsanstalt.

Lorenz, A. (2016). Freiwillige Souveränitätsabgabe? Kooperation und Fusion von Brandenburg und Berlin. In A. Lorenz, A. Anter & W. Reutter, *Politik in Brandenburg* (pp. 227–446). Springer VS.

Lorenz, A., & Reutter, W. (2013). Subconstitutionalism in a multilayered system. A comparative analysis of constitutional politics in the German länder. *Perspectives on Federalism, 4*(2), 141–170. https://www.on-federalism.eu/attachments/141_download.pdf. Accessed 19 Dec 2019.

Lorenz, A., Anter, A., & Reutter, W. (2016). *Politik in Brandenburg.* Springer VS.

Marschall, S. (1999). *Öffentlichkeit und Volksvertretung. Theorie und Praxis der Public Relations von Parlamenten.* Westdeutscher Verlag.

Marschall, S. (2005). *Parlamentarismus. Eine Einführung.* Nomos.

März, P. (2006). Ministerpräsidenten. In H. Schneider & H.-G. Wehling (Eds.), *Landespolitik in Deutschland. Grundlagen—Strukturen—Arbeitsfelder* (pp. 148–184). VS Verlag.

Massing, P. (1990). Berlin. In F. Esche & J. Hartmann (Eds.), *Handbuch der deutschen Bundesländer* (pp. 133–170). Campus.

Merkel, W. (2011). Volksabstimmungen: Illusion und Realität. *Aus Politik und Zeitgeschichte, 61*(44–45), 47–55.

Merkel, W. (2019). „Demokratie wird zur Sache der Bessergestellten" (Interview). *Tagesspiegel* vom 18. November 2019. https://www.tagesspiegel.de/politik/die-spd-und-das-risiko-volksentscheid-demokratie-wird-zur-sache-der-bessergestellten/25238366.html. Accessed 21 Nov 2019.

Merkel, W., & Petring, A. (2011). *Demokratie in Deutschland 2011. Ein Report der Friedrich-Ebert-Stiftung. Partizipation und Inklusion.* https://www.wzb.eu/system/files/docs/dps/dd/partizipation_und_inklusion.pdf. Accessed 10 March 2020.

Möllers, C. (2008). *Die drei Gewalten. Legitimation der Gewaltengliederung in Verfassungsstaat, Europäischer Integration und Internationalisierung.* Velbrück.

Montesquieu, Charles-Louis de Secondat, Baron de la Brède et de (1979). *De l'esprit des lois 1* [1748]. Chronologie, introduction, bibliographie par Victor Goldschmidt. Flammarion.

Montesquieu, Charles-Louis de Secondat, Baron de la Brède et de (1994). *Vom Geist der Gesetze.* Auswahl, Übersetzung und Einleitung von Kurt Weigand. Philipp Reclam jun.

Möstl, M. (2005). Landesverfassungsrecht—zum Schattendasein verurteilt? Eine Positionsbestimmung im bundesstaatlichen und supranationalen Verfassungsverbund. *Archiv des öffentlichen Rechts, 130*(3), 350–391.

Münch, U. (2011). Die Initiativtätigkeit des Bundesrates im Wandel der Zeit. In S. Leunig & U. Jun (Eds.), *60 Jahre Bundesrat* (pp. 88–105). Nomos.

Münch, U. (2012). Politikwissenschaftliche Dimensionen von Entwicklung und Stand des bundesdeutschen Föderalismus. Grundlagen des Föderalismus und der deutsche Bundesstaat. In I. Härtel (Ed.), *Handbuch Föderalismus—Föderalismus als demokratische Rechtsordnung und Rechtskultur in Deutschland, Europa und der Welt* (Vol. I, pp. 179–196). Springer.

Münch, U. (2019). Die unterlaufenen Föderalismusreformen in Deutschland. In Europäisches Zentrum für Föderalismus-Forschung Tübingen (Ed.), *Jahrbuch des Föderalismus 2019. Föderalismus, Subsidiarität und Regionen in Europa* (pp. 53–66). Nomos.

Neumann, H. (2000). *Die Niedersächsische Verfassung. Handkommentar* (3rd ed.). Boorberg.

Niclauß, K. (1998). *Der Weg zum Grundgesetz. Demokratiegründung in Westdeutschland.* Schöningh.

Niedermayer, O. (1996). Zur systematischen Analyse der Entwicklung von Parteiensystemen. In O. W. Gabriel & J. W. Falter (Eds.), *Wahlen und politische Einstellungen in westlichen Demokratien* (pp. 19–49). Peter Lang.

Niedermayer, O. (1997). Das gesamtdeutsche Parteiensystem. In O.W. Gabriel, O. Niedermayer & R. Stöss (Eds.), *Parteiendemokratie in Deutschland* (pp. 106–130). Bundeszentrale für politische Bildung.

Niedermayer, O. (2013a). Die Analyse einzelner Parteien. In O. Niedermayer (Ed.), *Handbuch Parteienforschung* (pp. 61–82). Springer VS.

Niedermayer, O. (2013b). Die Analyse von Parteisystemen. In O. Niedermayer (Ed.), *Handbuch Parteienforschung* (pp. 83–118). Springer VS.

Niedermayer, O. (2013c). Die Parteiensysteme der Bundesländer. In O. Niedermayer (Ed.), *Handbuch Parteienforschung* (pp. 765–790). Springer VS.

Niedermayer, O. (2013d). Parteimitgliedschaften. In O. Niedermayer (Ed.), *Handbuch Parteienforschung* (pp. 147–177). Springer VS.

Niedermayer, O. (2015). Die brandenburgische Landtagswahl vom 14. September 2014: Die Linke wird abgestraft, bleibt aber Regierungspartei. *Zeitschrift für Parlamentsfragen, 46*(1), 21–38.

Niedermayer, O. (2019). Parteimitgliedschaften im Jahre 2018. *Zeitschrift für Parlamentsfragen, 50*(2), 385–410.

Nohlen, D. (2000). *Wahlrecht und Parteiensystem* (3rd ed.). Leske + Budrich.

Oberreuter, H. (1992a). Gesetzgebungsverfahren. In M. G. Schmidt (Ed.), *Die westlichen Länder. Lexikon der Politik* (Vol. 3, pp. 121–129). Beck.

Oberreuter, H. (1992b). Gewaltenteilung. In M. G. Schmidt (Ed.), *Die westlichen Länder. Lexikon der Politik* (Vol. 3, pp. 135–142). Beck.

Oberreuter, H. (1996). Was nicht in den Medien ist, ist nicht Wirklichkeit. Parlamente—Foren politischer Öffentlichkeit? In H. Oberreuter (Ed.), *Parlamentarische Konkurrenz? Landtag—Bundestag—Europaparlament. Colloquium II der Akademie für Politische Bildung Tutzing am 8. Februar 1996 in Bayreuth. Der Landtag als Forum der politischen Öffentlichkeit. Colloquium III der Akademie für Politische Bildung Tutzing am 25. April 1996 in Regensburg* (pp. 105–120). München.

Obrecht, M., & Haas, T. (2012). Der Landtag von Baden-Württemberg. In S. Mielke & W. Reutter (Eds.), *Landesparlamentarismus. Geschichte—Struktur—Funktionen* (pp. 67–104). VS Verlag.

Parlamentarischer Rat. (1974–1997). *Der Parlamentarische Rat 1948–1949. Akten und Protokolle*. Edited by Deutscher Bundestag and Bundesarchiv (Vols. 14). Harald Boldt Verlag.

Patzelt, W. J. (1995). *Abgeordnete und ihr Beruf. Interviews—Umfragen—Analysen*. Akademie Verlag.

Patzelt, W. J. (1996). Deutschlands Abgeordnete: Profil eines Berufsstandes, der weit besser ist als sein Ruf. *Zeitschrift für Parlamentsfragen, 27*(3), 463–502.

Patzelt, W. J. (1998a). Ein latenter Verfassungskonflikt? Die Deutschen und ihr parlamentarisches Regierungssystem. *Politische Vierteljahresschrift, 39*(4), 725–727.

Patzelt, W. J. (1998b). Wider das Gerede vom „Fraktionszwang"! Funktionslogische Zusammenhänge, populäre Vermutungen und die Sicht der Abgeordneten. *Zeitschrift für Parlamentsfragen, 29*(2), 324–346.

Patzelt, W. J. (2006). Länderparlamentarismus. In H. Schneider & H.-G. Wehling (Eds.), *Landespolitik in Deutschland. Grundlagen—Strukturen—Arbeitsfelder* (pp. 108–129). VS Verlag.

Pestalozza, C. (2014a). Einführung. In C. Pestalozza (Ed.), *Verfassungen der deutschen Bundesländer mit dem Grundgesetz* (10th ed., pp. XVII-CXLVII). Beck.

Pestalozza, C. (Ed.). (2014b). *Verfassungen der deutschen Bundesländer mit dem Grundgesetz* (10th ed.). Beck.

Petersen, T. (2019). Die Einstellung der Deutschen zum Föderalismus. In Europäisches Zentrum für Föderalismus-Forschung Tübingen (Ed.), *Jahrbuch des Föderalismus 2019. Föderalismus, Subsidiarität und Regionen in Europa* (pp. 113–126). Nomos.

Petersen, T., Scheller, H., & Wintermann, O. (2008). Public Attitudes towards German Federalism: A Point of Departure for a Reform of German (Fiscal) Federalism? Differences between Public Opinion and the Political Debate. *German Politics, 17*(4), 559–586. https://doi.org/10.1080/09644000802501638.

Pfetsch, F. R. (1985). *Verfassungspolitik der Nachkriegszeit. Theorie und Praxis des bundesdeutschen Konstitutionalismus*. Wissenschaftliche Buchgesellschaft.

Pfetsch, F. R. (1990). *Ursprünge der Zweiten Republik. Prozesse der Verfassungsgebung in den Westzonen und in der Bundesrepublik*. Westdeutscher Verlag.

Plöhn, J. (2020). Landesverfassungsgerichte und Landtagswahlen: Wahlrecht „ad libitum" oder unter „strict scrutiny"? In W. Reutter (Ed.), *Verfassungsgerichtsbarkeit in Bundesländern. Theoretische Perspektiven, methodische Überlegungen und empirische Befunde* (pp. 289–322). Springer VS.

Plöhn, J., & Barz, A. (1990). Saarland. In F. Esche & J. Hartmann (Eds.), *Handbuch der deutschen Bundesländer* (pp. 383–416). Campus.

Ragnitz, J. & Thum, M. (2019). Gleichwertig, nicht gleich. Zur Debatte um die „Gleichwertigkeit der Lebensverhältnisse. *Aus Politik und Zeitgeschichte, 69*(46), 13–18.

Rehmet, F. (2019). *Volksbegehrensbericht 2019. Direkte Demokratie in den deutschen Ländern 1946 bis 2018 von Mehr Demokratie e.V.* Berlin: Mehr Demokratie e.V. https://www.mehr-demokratie.de/fileadmin/pdf/Volksbegehrensbericht_2019.pdf. Accessed 27 Nov 2019.

Reichart-Dreyer, I. (2008). Das Parteiensystem Berlins. In U. Jun, M. Haas & O. Niedermayer (Eds.), *Parteien und Parteiensysteme in den deutschen Ländern* (pp. 147–166). VS Verlag.

Reiser, M. et al. (2019). *Politische Kultur im Freistaat Thüringen. Gesundheit und Pflege in Thüringen. Ergebnisse des Thüringen-Monitors 2019*. Jena. https://www.landesregierung-thueringen.de/fileadmin/user_upload/Landesregierung/Landesregierung/Thueringenmonitor/Thueringen-Monitor_2019_mit_Anhang.pdf. Accessed 5 Dec 2019.

Renner, V. (1958). Entstehung und Aufbau des Landes Baden-Württemberg. *Jahrbuch des öffentlichen Rechts der Gegenwart* (N.F), *7*, 197–233.

Renzsch, W. (2000): Bundesstaat oder Parteienstaat: Überlegungen zu Entscheidungsprozessen im Spannungsfeld von föderaler Konsensbildung und parlamentarischem Wettbewerb in Deutschland. In W. Holtmann & H. Voelzkow (Eds.), *Zwischen Wettbewerbs- und Verhandlungsdemokratie. Analysen zum Regierungssystem der Bundesrepublik Deutschland* (pp. 53–78). Westdeutscher Verlag.

Reus, I., & Vogel, S. (2018). Policy-Vielfalt zwischen den Bundesländern nach der Föderalismusreform I: Art, Ausmaß und Akteure. *Zeitschrift für Vergleichende Politikwissenschaft, 12*(4), 621–642.

Reutter, W. (2005). Vertrauensfrage und Parlamentsauflösung. Anmerkungen zur verfassungspolitischen Debatte und zur Verfassungspraxis in den Ländern. *Politische Vierteljahresschrift, 46*(4), 655–673.

Reutter, W. (2006). Föderalismusreform und Gesetzgebung. *Zeitschrift für Politikwissenschaft, 16*(4), 1249–1274.

Reutter, W. (2006). Regieren nach der Föderalismusreform. *Aus Politik Und Zeitgeschichte, 50*, 12–17.

Reutter, W. (2008). *Föderalismus, Parlamentarismus und Demokratie. Landesparlamente im Bundesstaat*. Budrich (utb).

Reutter, W. (2012). Das Abgeordnetenhaus von Berlin: Ein Stadtstaatenparlament im Bundesstaat. In S. Mielke & W. Reutter (Eds.), *Landesparlamentarismus. Geschichte—Struktur—Funktionen* (pp. 143–146). VS Verlag.

Reutter, W. (2013). *Zur Zukunft des Landesparlamentarismus. Der Landtag Nordrhein-Westfalen im Bundesländervergleich*. Springer VS.

Reutter, W. (2016a). Vizepräsidenten in Landesparlamenten. Eine Bestandsaufnahme aus Anlass einer Verfassungsänderung in Brandenburg. *Zeitschrift für Parlamentsfragen, 47*(3), 607–618.

Reutter, W. (2016b). Wahlen und Parteien in Brandenburg. In A. Lorenz, A. Anter & W. Reutter, *Politik und Regieren in Brandenburg* (pp. 59–72). Springer VS.

Reutter, W. (2017a). Landesparlamente im unitarischen Bundesstaat: „Machtlosigkeit" und „unheilige Allianz". *Österreichische Zeitschrift für Politikwissenschaft, 46*(4), 1–15. https://doi.org/10.15203/ozp.2390.vol46iss4.

Reutter, W. (2017b). Landesverfassungsgerichte in der Bundesrepublik Deutschland — eine politikwissenschaftliche Bestandsaufnahme. In W. Reutter (Ed.), *Landesverfassungsgerichte in der Bundesrepublik Deutschland. Entwicklung—Aufbau—Funktionen* (pp. 21–48). Springer VS.

Reutter, W. (2017c). Der Verfassungsgerichtshof des Landes Berlin. In W. Reutter (Ed.), *Landesverfassungsgerichte in der Bundesrepublik Deutschland. Entwicklung—Aufbau—Funktionen* (pp. 77–104). Springer VS.

Reutter, W. (2018a). Landesverfassungsgerichte: „Föderaler Zopf" oder „Vollendung des Rechtsstaates"? *Recht Und Politik, 54*(2), 195–207.

Reutter, W. (2018b). *Verfassungspolitik in Bundesländern. Vielfalt in der Einheit*. Springer VS.

Reutter, W. (2020a). Zum Status der Landesverfassungsgerichte als Verfassungsorgane. In W. Reutter (Ed.). *Verfassungsgerichtsbarkeit in Bundesländern. Theoretische Perspektiven, methodische Überlegungen und empirische Befunde* (pp. 155–174). Springer VS.

Reutter, W. (2020b). Verfassungsrichterinnen und Verfassungsrichter: zur personalen Dimension der Landesverfassungsgerichtsbarkeit. In W. Reutter (Ed.), *Verfassungsgerichtsbarkeit in Bundesländern. Theoretische Perspektiven, methodische Überlegungen und empirische Befunde* (pp. 203–233). Springer VS.

Reutter, W. (Ed.). (2020). *Verfassungsgerichtsbarkeit in Bundesländern. Theoretische Perspektiven, methodische Überlegungen und empirische Befunde.* Springer VS.

Reutter, W. (2021). Subnational Constitutionalism in Germany: Constitutional autonomy, unitarian federalism, and intertwined policy-making. In P. Popelier, N. Aroney & G. Delledonne (Eds.), *Routledge Handbook of Subnational Constitutions and Constitutionalism.* Routledge (in print).

Ruhm von Oppen, B. (Ed.). (1955). *Documents on Germany under Occupation, 1945–1954.* Oxford: Oxford University Press.

Rütters, P. (2012). Landesparlamentarismus—Saarland. In S. Mielke & W. Reutter (Eds.), *Landesparlamentarismus. Geschichte—Struktur—Funktionen* (pp. 471–508). VS Verlag.

Rytlewski, R. (1999). Berliner Politik: Zwischen Kiez und Stadtstaat. In W. Süß & R. Rytlewski (Eds.), *Berlin. Die Hauptstadt* (pp. 295–329). Bundeszentrale für politische Bildung.

Sachsen-Monitor (2018.). *Sachsen-Monitor 2018. Ergebnisbericht.* https://www.staatsregierung.sachsen.de/download/ergebnisbericht-sachsen-monitor-2018.pdf. Accessed 20 Nov 2019.

Scharpf, F. W. (1985). Die Politikverflechtungsfalle: Europäische Integration und deutscher Föderalismus im Vergleich. *Politische Vierteljahresschrift, 26*(4), 323–356.

Scharpf, F. W. (2009). *Föderalismusreform. Kein Ausweg aus der Politikverflechtungsfalle?* Campus.

Scharpf, F. W., Reissert, B., & Schnabel, F. (1976). *Politikverflechtung. Theorie und Empirie des kooperativen Föderalismus in der Bundesrepublik.* Scriptor.

Scheller, H. (2016). Der föderalismustheoretische Diskurs in der Bundesrepublik—zwischen Pfadabhängigkeit und normativer Verselbständigung. In E.M. Hausteiner (Ed.), *Föderalismus. Modelle jenseits des Staates* (pp. 51–78). Nomos.

Schmidt, M. G. (1980). *CDU und SPD an der Regierung. Ein Vergleich ihrer Politik in den Ländern.* Campus.

Schmidt, M. G. (1987). West Germany: The Politics of the Middle Way. *Journal of Public Policy, 7*(2), 139–177.

Schmidt, M. G. (1990). Die Politik des mittleren Weges. Besonderheiten der Staatstätigkeit in der Bundesrepublik Deutschland. *Aus Politik Und Zeitgeschichte,9–10,* 23–31.

Schmidt, M.G. (2000). *Demokratietheorien* (3rd ed.). Leske + Budrich (utb).

Schmidt, M.G. (2011). *Das politische System Deutschlands. Institutionen, Willensbildung und Politikfelder.* Beck.

Schmidt, T.I. (2012). Der Bundesrat. Geschichte, Struktur, Funktion. In I. Härtel (Ed.), *Handbuch Föderalismus—Föderalismus als demokratische Rechtsordnung und Rechtskultur in Deutschland, Europa und der Welt. Grundlagen des Föderalismus und der deutsche Bundesstaat* (Vol. 1, pp. 651–690). Springer.

Schmidt-Jortzig, E. (2012). „Abweichungsgesetzgebung" als neues Kompetenzverteilungsinstrument zwischen den Gliederungsebenen des deutschen Bundesstaates. Grundlagen des Föderalismus und der deutsche Bundesstaat. In I. Härtel (Ed.), *Handbuch Föderalismus—Föderalismus als demokratische Rechtsordnung und Rechtskultur in Deutschland, Europa und der Welt* (Vol. I, pp. 611–626). Springer.

Schmitt, C. (1988). *Die geistesgeschichtliche Lage des heutigen Parlamentarismus* [1923] (8th ed.). Duncker & Humblot.

Schneider, H. (1990). Baden-Württemberg. In F. Esche & J. Hartmann (Eds.), *Handbuch der deutschen Bundesländer* (pp. 53–90). Campus.

Schneider, H. (1997). Parteien in der Landespolitik. In O.W. Gabriel, O. Niedermayer & R. Stöss (Eds.), *Parteiendemokratie in Deutschland* (pp. 407–426). Bundeszentrale für politische Bildung.

Schneider, H. (2001). *Ministerpräsidenten. Profil eines politischen Amtes im deutschen Föderalismus.* Leske + Budrich.

Schneider, H., & Wehling, H.-G. (Eds.). (2006). *Landespolitik in Deutschland.* VS Verlag.

Schniewind, A. (2008a). Parteiensysteme. In A. Freitag & A. Vatter (Eds.), *Die Demokratien der deutschen Bundesländer* (pp. 63–110). Barbara Budrich.

Schniewind, A. (2008b). Regierungen. In A. Freitag & A. Vatter (Eds.), *Die Demokratien der deutschen Bundesländer* (pp. 111–160). Barbara Budrich.

Schniewind, A. (2012). *Die Parteiensysteme der Bundesländer im Vergleich: Bestandsaufnahme und Entwicklungen.* Lit.

Schüttemeyer, S.S. (1995). Repräsentation. In D. Nohlen & R.-O. Schultze (Eds.), *Politische Theorien. Lexikon der Politik* (Vol. 5, pp. 543–552). Beck.

Schüttemeyer, S.S., Kolkmann, M., & Lübker, M. et al. (1999). *Die Abgeordneten des Brandenburgischen Landtages: Alltag für die Bürger.* Landeszentrale für die politische Bildung.

Schwarz, K.-A. (2012). Länderneugliederungen—ein Beitrag zur Reform der bundesstaatlichen Ordnung? Grundlagen des Föderalismus und der deutsche Bundesstaat. In I. Härtel (Ed.), *Handbuch Föderalismus—Föderalismus als demokratische Rechtsordnung und Rechtskultur in Deutschland, Europa und der Welt* (Vol. I, pp. 593–607). Springer.

Schwarzmeier, M. (2001). *Parlamentarische Mitsteuerung. Strukturen und Prozesse informalen Einflusses des Bundestages.* Westdeutscher Verlag.

Simon, D. (2004). Rechtsverständlichkeit. In K.D. Lerch (Ed.), *Recht verstehen. Verständlichkeit, Missverständlichkeit und Unverständlichkeit von Recht* (pp. 405–412). de Gruyter.

Sörgel, W. (1985). *Konsensus und Interessen. Eine Studie zur Entstehung des Grundgesetzes.* Leske + Budrich.

Sontheimer, K., Bleek, W., & Gawrich, A. (2007). *Grundzüge des politischen System Deutschlands. Völlig überarbeitete Neuausgabe.* Piper.

Statistische Ämter der Länder. (2019). *Volkswirtschaftliche Gesamtrechnungen der Länder. Gesamtwirtschaftliche Ergebnisse im Bundesländervergleich.* Statistisches Landesamt Baden-Württemberg. https://www.vgrdl.de. Accessed 22 Nov 2019.

Statistisches Bundesamt. (2018). *Anzahl der Beschäftigten im öffentlichen Dienst in Deutschland nach Bundesländern am 30. Juni 2017.* Statista. Statista GmbH. Zugriff: 17. Dezember 2019. https://de.statista.com/statistik/daten/studie/36870/umfrage/oeffentlicher-dienst---beschaeft-igte-nach-bundeslaendern/. Accessed 15 Dec 2019.

Statistisches Bundesamt. (2019a). *Ausländische Bevölkerung nach Bundesländern.* https://www. destatis.de/DE/Themen/Gesellschaft-Umwelt/Bevoelkerung/Migration-Integration/Tabellen/auslaendische-bevoelkerung-bundeslaender.html. Accessed 26 Nov 2019.

Statistisches Bundesamt. (2019b). *Bevölkerung - Einwohnerzahl der Bundesländer in Deutschland am 31. Dezember 2018.* https://de.statista.com/statistik/daten/studie/71085/umfrage/verteilung-der-einwohnerzahl-nach-bundeslaendern/. Accessed 13 Jan 2020.

Statistisches Bundesamt (Statista). (2019c). *Religionszugehörigkeit der Deutschen nach Bundesländern im Jahr 2011.* https://de.statista.com/statistik/daten/studie/201622/umfrage/religionszugehoerigkeit-der-deutschen-nach-bundeslaendern/. Accessed 13 Jan 2020.

Statistisches Bundesamt (Destatis). (2019d). *Statistisches Jahrbuch. Deutschland und Internationales.* https://www.destatis.de/jahrbuch. Accessed 15 Dec 2019.

Statistisches Landesamt Berlin. (2006ff.). *Wahlen in Berlin 2006, 2011 und 2016. Bericht vom Landeswahlleiter bzw. der Landeswahlleiterin.* Statistisches Landesamt. https://www.berlin. de/wahlen/historie/berliner-wahlen/artikel.778846.php. Accessed 2 Dec 2019.

Statusbericht. (1957). Der Status des Bundesverfassungsgerichts. Material—Gutachten, Denkschriften und Stellungnahmen mit einer Einleitung von Gerhard Leibholz. *Jahrbuch des öffentlichen Rechts der Gegenwart (N.F.), 6,* 109–221.

Steffani, W. (1979). *Parlamentarische und präsidentielle Demokratie. Strukturelle Aspekte westlicher Demokratien.* Westdeutscher Verlag.

Steffani, W. (1990). Bund und Länder in der Bundesrepublik Deutschland. In F. Esche & J. Hartmann (Ed.), *Handbuch der deutschen Bundesländer* (pp. 37–52). Campus.

Steffani, W. (1999). Der parlamentarische Bundesstaat als Demokratie. *Zeitschrift für Parlamentsfragen, 30*(4), 980–998.

Steinberg, R. (1992). Organisation und Verfahren bei der Verfassungsgebung in den Neuen Bundesländern. *Zeitschrift für Parlamentsfragen, 23*(3), 497–516.

Stiens, A. (1997). *Chancen und Grenzen der Landesverfassungen im deutschen Bundesstaat der Gegenwart*. Duncker & Humblot.

Sturm, R. (2001). *Föderalismus in Deutschland. Beiträge zur Politik und Zeitgeschichte.* Landeszentrale für politische Bildungsarbeit.

Sturm, R. (2011). Verfassungsrechtliche Schuldenbremsen im Föderalismus. *Zeitschrift für Parlamentsfragen, 46*(3), 648–662.

Sturm, R. (2012). Zweite Kammern in Deutschland und Europa: Repräsentation, Funktion, Bedeutung. Grundlagen des Föderalismus und der deutsche Bundesstaat. In I. Härtel (Ed.), *Handbuch Föderalismus—Föderalismus als demokratische Rechtsordnung und Rechtskultur in Deutschland, Europa und der Welt* (Vol. I, pp. 723–742). Springer.

Sturm, R. (2015). *Der deutsche Föderalismus. Grundlagen—Reformen—Perspektiven.* Nomos.

Sturm, R., & Pehle, H. (2012). *Das neue deutsche Regierungssystem. Die Europäisierung von Institutionen, Entscheidungsprozessen und Politikfeldern in der Bundesrepublik Deutschland* (3rd ed.). Springer VS.

Thaysen, U., (2005). Landesparlamentarismus zwischen deutschem Verbundföderalismus und europäischem Staatenverbund: Lage und Leistung 1990–2005. In Thüringer Landtag (Ed.), *Der Thüringer Landtag und seine Abgeordneten 1990–2005. Studien zu 15 Jahren Landesparlamentarismus* (pp. 19–68). hain Wissenschaft.

Töller, A. E., & Roßegger, U. (2018). Auswirkungen der Abweichungskompetenz der Länder. Methodische Überlegungen und erste Resultate am Beispiel des Naturschutzrechts. *Zeitschrift für Vergleichende Politikwissenschaft, 12*(4), 663–682.

Träger, H., & Priebus, S. (Eds.). (2017). *Politik und Regieren in Sachsen-Anhalt.* Springer VS.

Vogel, H.-J. (1995). Die bundesstaatliche Ordnung des Grundgesetzes. In E. Benda, W. Maihofer & H.-J. Vogel (Eds.), *Handbuch des Verfassungsrechts. Teil 2* (2nd ed., pp. 1041–1102). de Gruyter.

WWehling, H.-G. (2004a). Baden-Württemberg. Nach Gestalt und Traditionen von großer Vielfalt. In. H.-G. Wehling (Ed.), *Die deutschen Länder. Geschichte, Politik, Wirtschaft* (3rd ed., pp. 17–34). Leske + Budrich.

Wehling, H.-G. (2004). *Die deutschen Länder. Geschichte, Politik, Wirtschaft* (3rd ed.). Leske + Budrich.

Wehling, H.-G. (2006). Landespolitik und Länderpolitik im föderalistischen System Deutschlands—zur Einführung. In H. Schneider & H.-G. Wehling (Eds.), *Landespolitik in Deutschland. Grundlagen—Strukturen—Arbeitsfelder* (pp. 7–21). VS für Sozialwissenschaften.

Weichlein, S. (2019). *Föderalismus und Demokratie in der Bundesrepublik.* Kohlhammer.

Weigl, M. (2017). Der Bayerische Verfassungsgerichtshof. In W. Reutter (Ed.), *Landesverfassungsgerichte. Entwicklung—Aufbau—Funktionen* (pp. 53–76). Springer VS.

Wettig, G. (1999). Berlin vor den Herausforderungen des Kalten Krieges 1945–1989. In W. Süß & R. Rytlewski (Eds.), Berlin. Die Hauptstadt (pp. 157–186). Bundeszentrale für politische Bildung.

Winterhoff, C. (2012). Blüten des Föderalismus in der Praxis—Anmerkungen eines Rechtsanwenders. In I. Härtel (Ed.), *Handbuch Föderalismus—Föderalismus als demokratische Rechtsordnung und Rechtskultur in Deutschland, Europa und der Welt* (Vol. II, pp. 249–264). Springer.